Military Architecture

Excursions into Architecture
Series Editor
David Braithwaite A.A.Dipl., A.R.I.B.A.

MILITARY ARCHITECTURE

Quentin Hughes

HUGH EVELYN, LONDON

First published in 1974 by
Hugh Evelyn Limited
9 Fitzroy Square, London W1P 5AH
© 1974, Quentin Hughes

Designed by Lawrence Edwards

SBN 238.78988.8
Printed in Great Britain by
Hazell Watson and Viney Limited
Aylesbury, Bucks

CONTENTS

ACKNOWLEDGEMENTS

I wish to express my thanks to the many people who have helped me in the preparation of this book.

In particular I am indebted to Their Excellencies the Ambassadors to Malta of France, Italy, and Western Germany, Brigadier Paul Ward, Captain I. Drummond, RN, Lieutenant Colonel Marsh, RE, Lieutenant Colonel F. T. Stear, RE, and the staff at the library of the Royal Engineers' Institution, Major R. A. Bartelot, RA, and the staff of the Royal Artillery Institution, Captain P. Truttman and his colleagues in the French army at Thionville and Metz, Captain G. Koppert and his associates in the Dutch army at Utrecht, Mr and Mrs R. Blijstra, Mr Aulis Blomstedt, Professor J. P. Bonta, Mr David Dean, Dr C. J. Duffy, Mr J. V. H. Eames, Mrs Eva Friis, Dr De Pasquale and Chevalier Joseph Galea at the Royal Malta Library, Mr F. S. Mallia and Father Marius Zerafa at the National Museum in Valletta, Mr Caruana Dingli at the Department of the Environment, Malta, Mr R. Vella Bonavita, Dr Paul Xuereb, Mr John Mangion, Mr Frans Attard and students in the Department of Architecture at the Royal University of Malta. Mr David Braithwaite has painstakingly read and advised me on the text.

The photographs of Chester (p. 19), Restormel Castle (p. 24), Deal (p. 98), St Mawes and Pendennis Castles (p. 99) were kindly supplied by Aerofilms Ltd; those of the Tower of London (p. 25), Caerlaverock (p. 42), Claypots (p. 96) and Fort Tilbury (p. 148) by the Department of the Environment; Verdala Palace (p. 94) by Mr D. M. Wrightson; Naarden (p. 137) by KLM Aerocarto; Fort Popton (p. 190) by BP Ltd; Castello di San Marcos (p. 144) by United States National Parks Service; Monbeltrán (p. 52), Medina del Campo (p. 53), and Coca (p. 54) by Mr Alberto Weissmüller from his book *Castles from the Heart of Spain*, Barrie & Jenkins, London 1969, and Fort George (p. 150) by *The Scotsman*.

Finally I am most grateful to Mr Carmel Gatt and Mr Anton Valentino for help with the numerous line drawings in the text, to Miss Maria Cremona for interpreting my notes and typing my manuscript, and to my wife and my mother for their constant help.

PREFACE

'Military engineering,' wrote the eminent seventeenth century Marshal Vauban, 'is a business beyond our strength; it embraces too many things for a man to be able to make himself perfectly master of it.' In the succeeding three centuries the complexity of the art has increased threefold. What has been difficult to practise is as difficult to describe and write about. Perhaps this is why there is no comprehensive survey of the subject in any language, and why this book can only attempt to demonstrate the scope of the subject. There are many over-simplifications and numerous omissions and for this I apologise making only the excuse that with so massive a subject the references have had to be selective.

The main fascination of military architecture lies in its honesty. Admittedly there are elements of façadism applied purely for their psychological impact, like the ornate decoration of fortified gates and the rusticated walls which suggest a strength greater than they possess, but military architecture is essentially functional architecture; it has always had to be. For its efficient function it required an integrity of plan and section, the use of appropriate first rate materials and craftsmanship, and the strongest and most resistant forms of construction.

Its fascination also lies in its sculptural quality. It was Lendy who wrote, 'a thorough engineer sees his fortress completely modelled on a plateau, a hill, a plain, or a rock, just as a sculptor sees his statue in a block of marble; nay, more, he also makes the best of nature's resources'.

Equally one can say that its fascination lies in its very changing nature. Fontenelle called it the most difficult of all arts, 'since it does not afford to men of ordinary capacity the convenience of the application of certain fixed rules, but demands at every moment the natural and improved parts of a lofty genius'. Not subject to caprice or fashion, it has changed of necessity and has been forced to change in order to survive. It is an art with few vagaries. Nevertheless there have been rules and a pattern of evolution which is easier for us to see looking at the subject in retrospect. If a genius like Vauban could write, 'the art of fortifying does not consist in rules and systems, but solely in good sense and experience', other lesser mortals were in dire need of guidelines. One is reminded of the prisoner who had scrawled on the walls of his cell, 'Stone walls and iron bars do not a prison make, *but they sure help.*'

The evolution of military architecture is moulded by the weapons used against it and by those used in its support. Gradually weapons assumed a position of importance far in excess of the actual structure of the fort, and changes in fortification have been largely the consequence of improvements that have been made in weaponry. From earliest times the gun has in its various forms been the decisive factor in fortification. Its impact has been affected by its range, its energy and its mobility. Up to the fourteenth century the ancient and medieval ballistae were the main weapons of attack and defence, and engineers evolved with no great difficulty defences of sufficient strength to withstand attack. Soon the artillery cannon began to usurp the position of importance. By 1327 it was being used in siege warfare, and at the Battle of Crecy in 1346 was in action in the field. The efficiency of the cannon and of other weapons was then built up with ever-increasing momentum: wheeled artillery, flintlock muskets in 1521, mortars in 1543, the socket bayonet in 1702, the simplification and standardisation of gunparts by Gribauval in 1763 which soon led to mass production, shrapnel fire in 1810, explosive shells from 1826, breech-loading guns in the 1850s, machine guns in the 1870s, high explosive shells in 1885, quick-firing guns two years later and the magazine rifle in the following year, and the introduction of smokeless powder by 1890. From stone projectiles, the missiles changed to cast-iron shot fired from smoothbore ordnance, and finally to the introduction of missiles for rifled guns in 1859. The result was that muzzle energy increased at a phenomenal rate which, coupled with an increased weight of projectiles and a greater penetrating power, changed the pattern of war. The effective breaching range of a gun was increased from a mere 350 metres in the case of a 20-pounder in the sixteenth century to some 3,500 metres by the end of the nineteenth.

Throughout history there was a continual swing in the balance of the superiority of attack and defence. From a situation during the Middle Ages when defences were clearly superior and castles safe, an equilibrium was reached between attack and defence in the middle years of the sixteenth century, to be superseded by a superiority of attack over defence as a result of Vauban's innovations towards the end of the seventeenth century. From then on the situation fluctuated, sometimes the defences were proof against assault and in other periods they crumbled with surprising rapidity.

The trace or outline of the fortification was the result of the pressures imposed upon it, and as pressures changed so did the shape of the trace. Before 1480 height, thickness and solidity were sufficient barriers to aggression, but the invention of gunpowder rapidly changed the situation. In the old castles frontal fire, consisting of projectiles dropped from the walls or stone missiles thrown directly forward, was usually sufficient reply to any attack. By the early sixteenth century it became necessary to introduce a bastion system of defence, where the ground in front of a fortress was criss-crossed with fire through which any attacker must pass. As the range of weapons increased, defences had to be spread farther out into the countryside. As the striking power of missiles increased, defences had to be designed with a reduced profile and curved or angled surfaces to deflect their blows. The defences were thus thrown farther and farther out like an explosion, the parts fragmented and yet mutually related. The enlarged circumference and the high cost of building militated against the use of concentric circles of continuous fortifications stretching out like ripples in a pool. Detached forts became a substitute for a continuous enceinte. So the pattern was elaborated.

But an introduction is not the place to tell the story. The body of the text and the illustrations related to it must do that. A word of warning is necessary, however, before a reader unaccustomed to the subject ventures into the text. 'As among seamen,' wrote Sir William Chambers, 'there is a technical language, of which no admiral could be ignorant, without appearing ridiculous; so in architecture, and the professions connected therewith, there are particular modes of expression, and terms of art, of which an architect must by no means be ignorant.' Over the centuries military architecture has evolved a language of its own. In order to express succinctly the intricate techniques which have been introduced into the art it was necessary to evolve a large number of specialist words. An explanation of these is necessary if the subject is to be understood. For this reason a glossary has been included near the end of the book which should be sufficient to explain the words used in the text. The contents of the bibliography have created a more difficult problem. Books and articles on military architecture fill many volumes. Only those which have been found relevant to the writing of this book have been included, in the hope that they may provide sources of reference for those who wish to study further.

I close the introduction with a reminder that this subject is not of a warlike and provocative nature, rather it is the very essence of peaceful co-existence. Fortresses were designed to maintain authority, not to usurp it. Military architecture is the art of defence, not of attack. Permanent fortifications are in essence non-aggressive and unprovocative.

Quentin Hughes
Malta 1972

8

Chapter one

THE ANCIENT WORLD

From earliest times man has learnt to protect himself by artificial means. Unlike other animals which depend upon the slow evolution of natural protective devices, he has learnt to clothe his naked body, to warm himself by fire, to protect himself with weapons and secure himself and his possessions with an artificial protective screen which may be termed military architecture.

By the third millennium some cities in Mesopotamia were being fortified, mainly those of the smaller nations in an attempt to ward off the aggressive Assyrians. Walls of brick and stone were built thick and high in a bid to out-top the scaling ladders of attackers. Correspondingly the Assyrians pushed forward the techniques of attack and siege warfare. They breached walls and gates, tunnelled under them in order to make them collapse, scaled them with ladders and carried ramparts by direct assault. In these ways the Assyrians co-ordinated their techniques of attack. Large cumbersome battering-rams, about five metres long, running on six wheels, and resembling some ancient tank, were surmounted by a round turret about six metres high from which archers could give covering fire. The head of the ram could pierce joints in masonry and, by leverage, could slowly cause a wall to crumble.

In ancient Greece the stronger cities were placed high on invulnerable sites. The fortifications of Mycenae and Tiryns both date from about 1500 BC. At Mycenae the acropolis, on a naturally strong hillside, was surrounded by a wall of massive hewn masonry, a continuous enceinte without towers. The stronghold was approached from the lower city by a ramp and a passage leading through a double system of gateways; the impressive capital Gate of the Lions, with its monolithic jambs, marking the first entrance to the acropolis. The plan form of the citadel was irregular as the walls followed the naturally strong line of the ridge.

At Tiryns the hill rose in two stages, enveloped in a cyclopean masonry wall some nine metres thick and about 20 metres high. It was a long finger of a city with a crosswall cutting off the citadel on the higher ground from the lower ward. High massive walls along the escarpment were the defence of this stronghold. The path was a ramp fashioned so that visitors were forced to expose the right side of their bodies unprotected by their shields as they approached the city walls. Only if he passed through three gateways, each at right angles to the last and with no space in which to charge, could any assailant penetrate the main rooms of the palace.

The Euryalus castle, standing on the western edge of a

The Walls of Mycenae and (below)
the fortified walls of Tiryns; after
Perrot and Chipiez

limestone ridge five miles from the centre of Syracuse, is probably the most complete Greek fortress remaining. It was begun by Dionysius I (405–367 BC) but the work was spread over a long period. Modifications were probably still being undertaken by Archimedes when the Romans under Marcellus besieged the fort and sacked the city in 212 BC. Commanding the plains and the road to the centre of Sicily, the fortress projected from the extremity of the town walls like a 'broad nail' along the high salient ridge. Facing the probable direction of attack there were three deep ditches, the centre and the innermost being inter-connected by a series of underground passages probably designed to facilitate the removal of any earth on which attackers might attempt to cross the ditches, and so contrived that an enemy penetrating the subterranean passages was constantly forced to turn to his right thus exposing the unprotected part of his body. There were outworks between the ditches and a bold triangular ravelin was poised above the scarp of the inner ditch. Behind this ravelin stood five huge towers capable of housing heavy ballistae which could pour a devastating fire on to the extremity of the outer ditch. Beyond the ballistae lay the keep, a further enclosure containing the castle's wells and a strong tower at the junction with the city walls.

The development of the techniques of attack and defence went forward apace. Syracuse is credited with the invention of the catapult in 399 BC, a device which could throw stones and arrows with considerable force. The performance of this weapon was improved by the discovery of the principle of exploiting torsion, which was probably applied to catapults as early as 330 BC. Like many weapons of war its introduction frightened people and a contemporary writer, seeing cata-pult artillery in action for the first time, cried 'Man's martial valour is of no avail any more!' It was the moral effect of artillery which was most telling. As later, with the introduction of gunpowder, the possession of large artillery pieces improved the morale of troops and demoralised the enemy. But ancient artillery was also very accurate, and arrow-shooting and stone-throwing catapults could operate effectively up to about 400–500 metres. In an assault their main purpose was to neutralise the defence so that rams could be pushed forward to destroy the walls. In an attack artillery could be used to kill the defenders on a wall, to stop dead a sally from a town and for counter-battery work against machines mounted on the towers of a besieged town. In defence artillery provided covering fire in support of sallies and, placed in elevated situations on towers, was effective in counter-battery work against besiegers' guns. Already the principle of the tactical handling of artillery was emerging in a manner which has remained operative to this day.

The siege of Tyre by the army of Alexander the Great in 332 BC is a classic and well-recorded example of the outstanding ingenuity displayed by both attack and defence. Alexander benefited from the army reorganisation carried out by his father, Philip of Macedon, his build-up of elaborate siege machinery and the employment of first rate military engineers, but Tyre was a tough nut to crack. The Tyrians withdrew into their stronghold, a city perched on the edge of the sea and providing no firm ground for the erection of the Greeks' engines of attack. There seemed little to fear; Alexander had no navy then available, relief was expected from the Persian fleet and the city was considered impregnable. Alexander however was determined upon its capture and

A reconstruction of the Castello Eurialo at Syracuse by Luigi Mauceri

Underground passages leading to the ditch in the Castello Eurialo

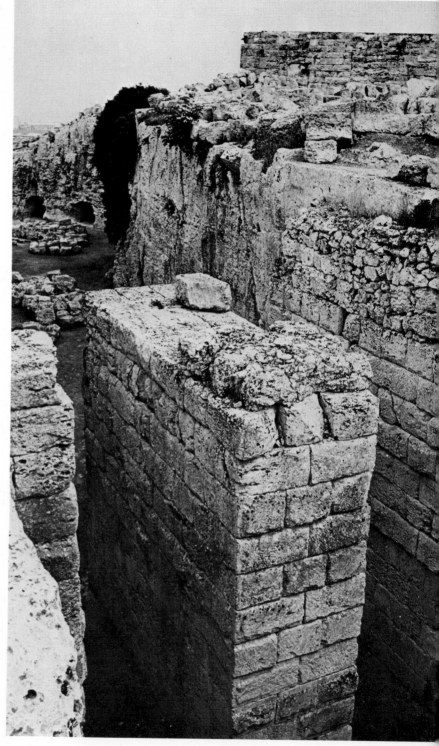

Castello Eurialo; massive abutments supported the ballistae

pushed forward his siege with painstaking care and detailed planning. A mole, some 66 metres wide, was built out towards the island site of the city and piles were driven into the muddy shore. As the mole was pushed nearer to the city walls, its workmen were constantly harassed by archers and slingers operating from their lofty positions. The Greeks retaliated by building two tall towers from which they suspended sails and the hides of animals wetted by seawater and soaked in vinegar in an attempt to make them fireproof, but the Tyrians fitted up a fireship filled with combustibles and with two masts projecting from its prow from which were suspended other highly inflammable materials. By loading the stern of the fireship its bows were made to rise high and, caught by the wind, the ship sped towards the mole, ramming the base of the towers which were soon ablaze. The defenders were either consumed by the flames or leapt to their deaths. Swimmers and divers then pulled up the stakes which protected the outer face of the mole and, in the heavy seas which followed, its stonework was swept away. Undeterred, Alexander ordered a new mole to be constructed. It was to be wider and to have more room for the employment of artillery. The Greeks next brought up ships and the investment of the city began, but the navy's task was not easy. In manoeuvring close to the city walls the ships ran on to underwater obstacles, and at anchor their cables were cut by daring commando raids from the town. During the heat of midday the ships themselves were attacked and many sunk by platoons of marines operating from small boats. At night the Greeks retaliated by bombarding the city from floating batteries, but a sudden storm tore their planks apart and many of the heavily armed soldiers fell into the sea.

A mobile Roman tower illustrated in a
sixteenth century edition of Vegetius

A precarious method of attacking an enemy
fortress; after Vegetius, 1585

The fortifications of a Roman town by Vitruvius; after Daniele Barbaro, 1567

Bottom
Reconstruction of a stone-throwing onager by Viollet-le-Duc

The assault on the walls finally began from the Greek towers and their artillery on the mole. But the citizens were equally ingenious. Leather bags filled with wet seaweed were suspended from the ramparts to absorb the blows from the large rocks which were flung against the walls. Great revolving machines, like flails, were placed on the walls and when these flails were rapidly rotated they intercepted the darts and missiles, deflecting them from the city. Grappling hooks on long ropes swung out to tear the Greek soldiers from their towers and drop their mangled bodies on the rocks below. Other soldiers were entangled in nets. Red hot sand poured from the battlements penetrated the armour of the assault troops causing them, in removing it, to expose themselves to the arrows of the defenders.

There were times when Alexander considered abandoning the siege, but finally he ordered the great assault, a combined operation from the sea and the mole. Ships with drawbridges, similar in concept to modern infantry landing craft, carried marines into the initial attack. Stone throwers bombarded and quaked the city walls and arrow-firing catapults put down a barrage of covering fire for the Greek assault battalions. The force of the attack was irresistible. Breaches opened and the Greeks poured into the city. There was no mercy shown. Buildings were put to the flame and their defenders to the sword; 8,000 fell at their posts and a further 2,000 were crucified as a gesture to appease Alexander's wrath; 30,000 were sold into slavery. The siege had lasted from the middle of January until the middle of July, six months of concentrated attack and defence.

The defensive system of the Greek cities developed slowly over the years and with it came the emergence in embryo of

A nineteenth century drawing of the Roman gate, the Porta Nigra at Trèves

two basic systems of design. The first was the idea of making a curtain wall less vulnerable by placing along it, at intervals, projecting towers from which flanking fire could be poured across the front of the vulnerable curtain. The distance between each pair of towers was dictated by the effective range of the weapons used to flank them. As the towers were pushed forward they became as vulnerable as previously the curtain walls had been and towers were thus designed to support each other so that adjoining towers could always fire on troops assaulting any particular tower. Towers began to be shaped so as to deflect the shot of besiegers' artillery.

By the fourth century BC there was a major revolution in Greek siege technique, largely occasioned by the introduction of the catapult. Towers were built higher so that a defender's artillery could outrange that of an attacker, and larger so that heavier and more numerous artillery pieces could be sited for defence. The casemate was introduced, a chamber within a tower which protected the artillery piece from bad weather, for catapults were susceptible to damp conditions. The pieces fired arrows through slits in the walls and their crews were protected by the masonry of the towers. The difficulty in using this sort of layout was always the restriction it imposed upon manoeuvrability and observation. For this reason the Greeks tended to use circular or semi-circular towers at the most exposed positions of the defensive wall. But they also built towers of pentagonal shape pointed towards the front like the later bastion. These had the advantage that an attacker's shot glanced off their oblique fronts. But because of their pointed shape no artillery in them could fire directly forward, so the towers had to be

adequately flanked from their neighbours.

The distinction between these angled towers and the true bastion introduced by Italian engineers at the end of the fifteenth century should be clearly understood. The true bastion was designed so that its faces were elongated from the flanks of its adjoining bastions and it was therefore fully protected by flanking fire. On the other hand the Greek towers were merely pointed to deflect projectiles. This is a misunderstanding which has dogged many of the arguments about the origin of the bastion and has caused at least one writer to suggest that the bastion was invented by the military engineer of the Knights of St John at Rhodes about 1496, when, in fact, his work merely consisted of a Greek-type tower transmitted by succeeding generations of Romans, Byzantines and Saracens to the Knights at Rhodes.

There were ancient Greek examples of superimposed casemates where towers could bring a maximum of defensive fire to bear on any threatened front. This was really the birth of the idea which developed into those nineteenth century multi-gun artillery towers which can still be seen in places like Linz and Verona.

The first development then was the introduction of a system of flanking fire from well-designed projecting towers for the defence of a city wall. It was not necessarily a Greek invention, but certainly Greek engineers utilised this method of defence.

The second development, which has remained one of the basic principles to the present day, was the idea of defence in depth. It is known that at the siege of Syracuse between 213 and 211 BC Archimedes placed his military engines in front of the main wall of the city and had them covered by outworks. This increased their range and effectiveness against assaulting troops and allowed defenders on the outermost city walls to provide covering fire to ensure protection of the artillery. This was the basis of concentric defence which was fully utilised in the Theodosian Walls of Constantinople, the crusader castles in the Holy Land and the frontier forts of Edward I in Wales. The outworks were important and had to be strong. They were adequately provided with ditches, palisades and minefields. Pots filled with seaweed sufficiently compacted to withstand a man's weight, but which would collapse under the weight of an attacker's machines, were buried in the ground. The anti-tank trap is a modern equivalent. The use of all these devices became common practice under the Romans who, if not brilliant technical innovators, were extremely clever at adapting others' ideas.

Only large powerful cities and strategic strongholds could afford to ring themselves with defensive walls. Villages had to withstand threats as best they could, and it may be that the apparently haphazard irregular planning of some ancient villages was the result of a conscious attempt to confuse and bewilder any attacker who penetrated them. The Second World War demonstrated the difficulty of permeating dense urban areas and the comparative ease with which house to house fighting could hold up an apparently more powerful attacker. Witness the four week survival of the Jews in the Warsaw ghetto against great German superiority in equipment. Villages and small towns were often designed with a series of cul-de-sacs and alleys running at right angles to each other and terminating at a distance of one building-depth from the outer houses of the town. The latter, a continuous block of buildings constructed with blank outer walls, formed a dense defensive belt against attack from the surrounding countryside. Plato hints at this form of design where, by constantly closing the vista of town streets, strangers penetrating the maze were left confused. Thucydides describes how the Thebans lost their way in the narrow streets of Plataea and were surrounded by the villagers who, knowing all the intricacies of their town's layout, were able, unseen, to break through the party walls of their own houses and destroy the attackers. Remnants of this pattern of defence, both the unwindowed outer walls of houses and the apparent confusion of the cul-de-sac system, can be seen today in some of the villages of Malta.

The manner in which the Romans defended their towns is evident from numerous excavations and in the writings of two important authors on the art of fortification, Vitruvius and Vegetius. Neither author possessed much originality and both drew heavily on Greek inspiration, but their writings are important for they contain first hand knowledge of the aims and ideas of the Roman military engineer. Vitruvius was the first man to write about the use of symbolism as a means of promoting defence, the psychological impact of using architectural devices such as the caryatid. Women with burdens placed upon their heads were to show to posterity the punishment and humiliation which would be meted out to those who failed to defend their city and who conspired with an enemy. Similarly, there had been the representation of captive Persians to arouse patriotism for the defence of freedom among the Greek states. Just as the dangers of defeat could be represented by architectural devices, a feeling of strength could be imparted to a defensive

*Model in the Grosvenor Museum of the
Roman fortress at Chester*

The Roman walls at Portchester; plan

system in order to deter an attacker. The deterrent effect of military architecture has always been one of its most attractive constituents. The Romans often applied rusticated masonry to the towers which flanked the entrances to their towns. Not that rusticated stonework is stronger than ashlar; it is in fact weaker and more liable to be prised apart by attackers' rams, but its rugged quality gives the appearance of power; it looks stronger.

Vitruvius stated the principle which had been applied on the approach route to the citadel at Tiryns. 'As troops approach,' he wrote, 'their right side will be next to the wall and will not be protected by their shields.' His most important recommendation was that, in order to be most easily defensible, a city should be round in plan. An angular city, because some of its walls could obscure an attack from the

view of some of its defenders, helped an enemy. This suggestion was entirely at variance with Roman usage where the square or rectangular plan became the almost universal solution for fortresses and marching camps. Vitruvius took the principle even further, suggesting that towers also should be round so that an enemy could be seen from several sides. Towers were to be placed a bowshot apart and curtain walls were to be separated from towers by removable wooden planks so that, should attackers gain a foothold on one of the curtains, they would not be able to exploit this by passing their troops around the circuit of the walls. Each tower could be isolated and become a strongpoint even if surrounded by the enemy. Also, round or polygonal towers were better than square ones because the angles of square towers could be broken by battering-rams. In the case of round surfaces,

Portchester Castle

even when rams were driven wedge-fashioned towards the centre, they could not significantly damage the masonry. To further strengthen the defences, foundations were to be run out at right angles to the walls like the teeth of a comb.

Vitruvius' tenth book was about military machines and from this can be gathered much knowledge on the artillery of the ancient world. He described the sizes of catapults or scorpions and the methods of stringing and tuning them. He described the capstans, drums, blocks and pulleys of the giant ballistae and he outlined the method of using battering-rams and similar machines. There were machines for boring holes, others for scaling walls. A large wheeled tower, 20 storeys high, had an archers' gallery round each storey. Also there was a tortoise whose purpose was filling ditches in order to make it possible to breach the main wall of a besieged city. To resist blows and ward off fire the tortoise was covered with a double layer of stitched rawhide stuffed with seaweed or straw soaked in vinegar. The tortoise designed by Hegator of Byzantium was an immense affair weighing 218,000 kilogrammes, controlled by 100 men and fitted with an iron-pointed ram to breach walls. By the fourth century AD a new weapon, the onager, a single-armed military engine capable of throwing large stones with great accuracy, was in use.

Two of the greatest sieges in the history of the Roman army, at Avaricum and Alesia, were undertaken by Caesar in his campaign to subjugate Gaul between 58 and 50 BC. A reliable account of Roman siege methods described by Caesar himself has survived. Basically the procedure consisted of constructing a double belt of fortifications, the inner one completely enclosing the enemy city and sufficiently strong to prevent its forces breaking out; the outer belt was directed towards the open country in order to deny help from a relief force and to safeguard the rear of the besieging army.

Roman fortresses were of two kinds, the marching camp and the legionary fortress, and both were based on a gridiron plan of streets. In a legionary fortress the two main streets met at right angles in the centre of the fortress in front of the principia or headquarters of the legion, and at the extremities of the streets stood the city gates. The legionary fortress, from which many of the planned Roman towns developed, was surrounded by a rectangular or square enceinte with its corners slightly rounded, its walls sometimes punctuated at regular intervals by towers and its gateways supported by pairs of strong towers with casemates. The ramparts were sufficiently wide and deep for the employment of artillery. The plan was therefore quite different from Vitruvius' ideal circular solution for a city. Novaesium (Neuss) on the Rhine opposite Düsseldorf is the most completely excavated example and there are other fine remains at Chester and Caerleon. The earthen ramparts at Chester were some 8·5 metres wide at the base and 5·5 metres high to the terreplein, which was sufficiently wide for the easy movement of troops protected by an ample parapet. The construction of a legionary fortress was reinforced by turf laid on logs which were strapped together. At a later date an outer skin of stone was applied to form a more permanent defence line and towers were inserted at intervals. Beyond the ramparts lay a ditch, usually with a steep counterscarp, augmented by a thorn hedge barrier so that enemy troops penetrating the ditch would find their retreat impeded by sharp thorns as they stood exposed to retaliatory fire from the walls.

The other type of Roman fortress, either an auxilliary fort or a marching camp, was usually smaller, although laid out in the same basic gridiron plan and surrounded by a rectangular rampart. Marching camps protected the legions in hostile countries. Turf ramparts about 1·5 metres high, thrown up from the material of an encircling ditch, provided a protective screen for an encamped legion sheltered in its leather tents. The gateways were usually protected by a curved extension, a device which developed in the seventeenth century into the hornwork of the Vauban period, intended to force any attackers to approach the camp on an oblique line with their right sides exposed to the defenders' fire.

Auxiliary forts were placed at vulnerable points in the countryside to ward off sudden attack. Two of the best groups exist in Britain. Along the east and south coasts, from Norfolk to Hampshire, a chain of forts, called the 'forts of the Saxon Shore', nine of which have survived, were constructed in the third century AD. This was the first major coastal defence system in Britain, all the forts being placed at strategic points such as harbours or river mouths. The forts were mostly rectangular in plan, surrounded by high massive stone walls with circular towers projecting at intervals and sufficiently large for mounting ballistae. Portchester, near Portsmouth, is a well-preserved example. Once a large square Roman fort, the sides of which measured nearly 180 metres, it had 20 rounded towers placed at regular intervals, each one hollow with floors of timber capable of carrying light ballistae, and open to the interior of the fort. The towers at the corners were set diagonally. In the early middle ages, possibly in the reign of Henry I, a large square keep and its attendant castle were built into the north-west corner of this Roman fort.

The south coast forts were originally thought to be part of a defensive system constructed against Saxon sea raiders, but a recent theory has been advanced which suggests that they may have been built by Carausius, a Roman naval officer who had mutinied against imperial rule and wished to protect himself against a possible Roman counter-attack by the fleet of Maximian.

In the north of Britain there remains the most dramatic expression of Roman defensive architecture. Hadrian's Wall marks the northernmost limit of the Roman Empire. In about the year 122 the emperor ordered the construction of this mighty barrier stretching from coast to coast, over 120 kilometres long and some 4·5 metres high, with a 2 metre parapet originally designed to be about 3 metres wide. In front, where the ground was particularly vulnerable to an attack, a ditch some 8 metres wide, dug to an average depth of 2·7 metres, gave further protection. Guard rooms or mile castles were placed every mile along the wall with two guard turrets between each. Behind the wall ran a military road for the rapid movement of garrison troops stationed in 17 strategic forts stretching from Newcastle to the Solway Firth.

These latter forts were rectangular in plan and straddled the wall so that their northern front projected into the open country beyond. The gates were strongly fortified by supporting artillery towers, two of which lay astride the wall. This was the solution in forts like Benwell and Chesters, though others had their northern walls formed from the wall itself. At each end the two coasts were guarded by watch-towers and protected by additional forts to prevent an enemy outflanking the wall.

Chapter two

CASTLES OF THE MIDDLE AGES

The battle of Adrianople was fought in 378. Not only was it the most fearful defeat suffered by the Roman army for nearly 600 years, but it saw the demise of the Roman infantry and changed the whole pattern of warfare. Cavalry, forerunner of the armoured knights of the middle ages and the crusades, became the main striking force of an army in the field. Infantry, its role now subordinated, garrisoned the forts and castles in the years that followed. Infantry soldiers began to discard their heavy armour which was no match against the terrific impact of the mail-clad horse and rider. The power of the infantry soldier did not return until, in the fourteenth and early fifteenth centuries, he developed a means of defending himself with missiles. It will be recalled that British archers at Crecy and Agincourt were able to break a powerful cavalry charge before it could get near to them: at Laupen in 1339 Swiss pikemen, using long pointed weapons which outreached the horsemen's swords and maces, perfected an alternative method of breaking the power of cavalry.

In the meantime a new system of defence was evolved. Mobile armour was used to break an enemy, and feudal castles (that is, strongholds held by an occupying power) were used to hold down a subjugated race. This is what happened in Britain. William the Conquerer's cavalry, admittedly with considerable difficulty, finally shattered the English infantry at Hastings and William's followers then set in train a systematic occupation of the country. Hundreds of castles of subjugation were built. At first these Norman strongholds consisted of a motte and bailey, the motte being a mound of earth surrounded by a protective wooden palisade which, with the passage of time and the availability of money, was rebuilt as a strong stone wall, then called a shell-keep. There are many well-preserved examples, among the best being Launceston and Restormel castles in the west country. The motte became the strongroom of the castle, a prison for captives and a safe retreat for its lord. When built of stone it was fireproof. The bailey was more spacious, providing accommodation in peacetime and a refuge for animals and tenants in time of attack. The building of this type of castle at Hastings is illustrated on the Bayeux tapestry.

The massive square stone keeps are among the glories of Norman architecture, built so strongly that many have survived almost intact. The construction of the main ones was supervised by Gundulf, Bishop of Rochester from 1077 to

Restormel Castle

1108. He had taken part in a crusade and possibly had seen the Byzantine citadel at Saône, for its dimensions are close to those of the Tower of London's White Tower and the heavy buttresses resemble those at Colchester. The White Tower, now the central core of the Tower of London, was built by William the Conqueror to protect and control the city. Approximately square in plan, its battlements rise to a height of 27·5 metres, the walls some 4·5 metres thick at the base. To further strengthen this structure a thick crosswall was constructed the full height of the building, and a second massive wall cuts off from the rest of the keep the chapel of St John and its crypts, the apsidal projection of which can be seen on the outside of the building.

Rochester Castle on the old Roman road from the coast to London is mentioned in the Domesday Book. Part of the

The Tower of London (Crown Copyright)

castle was built by Gundulf about 1087 but the dominant keep-tower, the most splendid in Britain, was added about 1127 during the reign of Henry I. Rochester Castle was involved in three major sieges and still stands today. King John's siege of 1215 was described by a contemporary chronicler as follows: 'Our age has not known a siege so hard pressed nor so strongly resisted'. During the Barons' Wars it resisted siege engines until relieved by the king. The keep is square, 21·3 metres across at ground level, strengthened by a splayed base, and measuring 34·5 metres to the top of the parapet. The corners are strengthened by towers which rise a further 3·6 metres. Originally timber hoarding was cantilevered and roofed over so that archers could fire and drop missiles from a protected position. Like the Tower of London it has an internal crosswall which divides the interior.

The Norman keep at Rochester Castle

Below and right
Dover Castle

Dover Castle, called by Matthew Paris in the thirteenth century 'the key to England', is on a naturally strong site guarding the harbour. Probably the strongest castle in the country, its main buildings date from the reign of Henry II (1154–89). It was immensely expensive, costing about £7,000 and only rivalled by Richard I's castle at Château-Gaillard. The royal revenue was then only £10,000 a year. The keep, built between 1181 and 1188, was designed by Maurice the Engineer who may also have been responsible for Newcastle-on-Tyne keep. Although conservative in design, the general concept of Dover Castle is advanced. It was the first castle in western Europe which convincingly employed a concentric system of defence. This system, consisting of two independent defensive walls, had been used on the Theodosian Line at Constantinople in the fifth century. At Dover the inner curtain, probably begun in 1185, overshadows the outer curtain, whose defenders were thus covered from above. The outer curtain, thrust forward, took the brunt of an attack and held it at arm's length from the stronghold. Flanking towers project at intervals along both curtain walls, a device re-introduced by Henry II at Orford Castle but used much earlier by the Romans at places like Portchester.

Many of the Norman keeps were retained in castles which grew around them, and some were modified and embellished to provide more up to date accommodation. Of these latter Kenilworth is an example. It has aptly been described as looking like a burnt out factory, but it must have been magnificent in its heyday, embellished by the Earl of Leicester and containing John of Gaunt's hall which, after Westminster, was the finest in the land. A richly ornamental garden gave a sense of spaciousness conducive to gracious living. Kenilworth Castle dates from Norman times. The great square keep was once stark and forbidding, with small slits piercing its thick masonry. Leicester cut spacious windows in it to throw sunlight into the interior and parliamentarians blew out its rear wall when it succumbed, like so many English castles, to the cannon of the Civil War.

Few kings, except perhaps Edward I of England, have rivalled Frederick II as castle builders. Hohenstaufen Emperor of the West and King of Sicily, Frederick, in the year 1220, initiated a policy of pulling down all private castles in his domain in Italy and building a series of magnificent royal strongholds. Interested in architecture himself, his Swabian castles show a consistency which he may have inspired for they are clear statements of regal power, well-proportioned and symmetrical in plan. Castel del Monte in Apulia is the most beautiful. The octagonal castle, with its eight sturdy octagonal towers projecting clearly beyond the curtain wall, was intended to act as a central keep on high ground surrounded by a second peripheral curtain wall which was never built. Frederick's love of classical art is reflected not only in the symmetry of the plan, but in the pilastered and pedimented main doorway. There may also have been some influence from the Holy Land as the emperor undertook a crusade in 1227. There are French affinities too, especially in the similarity of the plan form to that of the castle at Boulogne (1231), Castel del Monte dating from about 1240. Some eight years later Frederick began the castle at Prato, a square

Right and opposite
Castel del Monte

plan with massive square corner towers and intermediate curtain towers, two of which are pointed or angular-shaped, perhaps a conscious revival of Greek and Roman forms. The tops of the walls and towers are battlemented, their parapets pierced by crenelles and protected by Guelph merlons of a later period, showing a characteristic zigzag silhouette against the sky.

In south-eastern Italy there are other castles of the period built by Frederick, Bari, Trani, Lucera, Termoli and Gioia del Colle, but their original outlines are partly obscured by later building. In troubled Sicily, seething with disorder, Frederick built his main strong castles, Syracuse, Augusta and, most imposing of all, the Castello Ursino at Catania. Catania, designed by Lentini and begun in 1239, combined the comfort of a royal residence with the requirements of defence. Symmetrical and mathematically precise, a vaulted perimeter of thick walls enclosed a square courtyard. There are four corner circular towers, and four semi-circular towers are placed centrally on the curtain walls. The concept is clearly Roman, but all of Frederick's castles show affinities to both Byzantine and Saracenic fortresses in the Middle East. Whether the Italian examples were derivative or shared a common source has not yet been convincingly established.

Although the First Crusade began in 1095 most of the significant castle-building in the Holy Land was undertaken later and was an extension of twelfth and thirteenth century architectural concepts in France. The influence of Byzantine castles must not, however, be underestimated, for Constantinople lay in the path of Geoffrey of Bouillon's First Crusade. Its fortifications stood intact with a landline dating from the time of Theodosius II (408–50), unbreached for a thousand years until it finally fell to the Turks in 1453. The Theodosian Walls stretched unbroken from the Golden Horn to the Sea of Marmara, a concentric line of defences pierced by seven main gates. The line was extremely strong, consisting of a main inner wall 4.5 metres thick and 12 metres high, with 96 projecting battlemented towers, some square, some octagonal, rising to a height of 18 metres. There was an open space, then the second wall between 7.5 and 9 metres high flanked by ten square towers, an outer esplanade 12 metres wide and a final defensive parapet. Beyond this lay the ditch, 18 metres wide and 6 metres deep, normally kept dry but capable of being flooded at short notice from the city's water supply. It was a most complex design of interrelated defences, each supporting its neighbour. There was nothing like it in the west and the city must have been a revelation to the crusader armies.

In the early years of the crusades the Franks, backed by a large army, had the initiative, but their strategy was poor. With their minds set upon the psychological victory of the capture of Jerusalem, both Aleppo and Damascus, a constant threat to their flank, were left unsubdued. Energy was dissipated and the christians carved out an impossibly shaped kingdom some 800 kilometres long and rarely more than 80

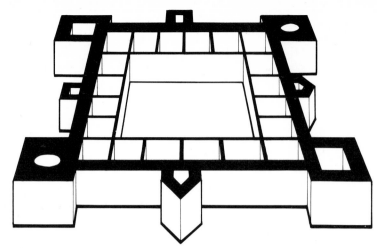

Below and right
Castello dell'Imperatore at Prato

Top and above
Castello Ursino at Catania in Sicily

Right
Margat Castle from the south-east; after Rey

Below right
Le Krak des Chevaliers; an aerial reconstruction by Sauvageot

Far right
View of Krak from the south-west; after Rey

to 96 kilometres wide. The long flank, instead of resting on the inhospitable sands of the desert, became in the years that followed a springboard for counter-attack by the Saracens. After the initial christian enthusiasm there was a continuous shortage of manpower, alleviated only temporarily by the army of the Third Crusade. Thus immense and strong fortifications were demonstrated to be pre-requisite to holding the New Kingdom. The castles constructed by the Templar and Hospitaller knights were the most powerful buildings of their time and they revolutionised military thinking in the west. The square keep was developed into a stronghold consisting of two or more linked towers, both a last line of defence in the event of a siege, and a highly protected core against any mutinous uprising of a mercenary garrison. The keep was ringed by concentric lines of curtain walls studded with round towers of deep salient capable of flanking the vulnerable curtains. Three or more tiers rose one above the other so that the archers with their now efficient bows could pour a devastating fire on an enemy. The old Greco-Roman device of exposing invaders to a series of right-angled turns in order to penetrate a castle gate was used. Machicolation was systematically developed into a corbelled timber parapet with holes in its floor through which stones and red hot material could be dropped on the attackers. Finally, the castle was thought of as a device for providing both active and passive defence. Posterns were provided so that the garrison could sally out and harass besiegers when they least expected it.

In peacetime the castles became the business and administrative centres of the land, controlling large highly efficient farms. In wartime their careful siting gave them control over each vulnerable pass and coastal anchorage, so that the castles stood like a chain along the length of the Holy Land. They were often grouped for interdependence and sited so that signals could be passed with great rapidity from one to another.

The greatest was Krak des Chevaliers, stronghold of the Knights of St John. It stood on a naturally defensible spur, watching over the Homs Gap. Only to the south was it vulnerable to direct assault and against this stood a massive keep of three linked towers standing above the castle's main reservoir, a deep water-filled moat. The knights took over an older castle on the same site and modified it in the 1140s, but the main work of construction was carried on after the earthquake of 1202 when complete redesigning took place. The plan was concentric with two tiers of curtain walls interspersed between projecting towers. The bases of the inner walls were further strengthened by a massive talus where the masonry was sloped outwards as protection against mining. The main entrance was in the eastern wall, approached up the steep scarp by a zigzag path which exposed an enemy to a barrage of missiles from the high walls. Each line of defence was supported by one above. 'A fortress, like a spiral spring, should offer more resistance the more it is compressed.' Krak was immensely strong and was never fairly taken. The Saracens attacked on at least 12 occasions and by 1271 it was held by no more than a skeleton garrison. Even then it fell as a result of cunning rather than by direct assault. A forged letter purporting to have come from the knights' headquarters induced its commander to lay down his arms and surrender his castle.

Krak, according to T. E. Lawrence, was 'the most wholly

Edward I's castle at Rhuddlan

admirable castle in the world'. There were many other significant bastions in the Holy Land, but there is only space for two references. Margat lies on the Syrian coast. An irregular fortress of considerable size, in 1186 it became the property of the Knights of St John who turned it into their headquarters. Its system of defence is less easily read than Krak, but the castle consists basically of a triangular citadel with a double perimeter of walls. Two of its corners are joined to an outer ward which is only partly concentric. Saône is more impressive, its walled enclosure occupying about five hectares on a narrow spit of land running from north-east to south-west and dropping on three sides into deep gorges. The ground is conveniently bisected to form a lower bailey on the promontory and an upper bailey with a keep formed from the old Byzantine castle. The north-east front is of necessity more strongly defended and here there is another deep ditch cut across the peninsula, with a tall needle of rock which rises 27 metres from the bed of the 18 metre wide ditch to support the bridge leading to the main gate. It is indeed forbidding and was only captured by Saladin in 1188 after heavy bombardment with mangonels against a garrison far too depleted to hold so large a perimeter.

In 1291 the knights withdrew to their base camp at Acre and, before a devastating attack, with all the paraphernalia of siege warfare, they made their last stand. After six weeks of siege they surrendered and withdrew for ever from the Holy Land.

The great works of Edward I in Wales are a culmination of the long line of development from Roman and Byzantine times. Like the Doric order, by fine adjustments over generations the medieval fortress was brought to a kind of perfection. Edward was probably the greatest castle builder in the middle ages. As a crusader he had strengthened the defences of Acre and, probably on his return home in 1273, had commissioned James of St George from Savoy to carry out his projects. His work in Britain falls into three periods. In the initial campaign to bottle up the Welsh in their mountain fastness Edward ordered the building of castles and towns to secure his lines of communication. He had control of the sea and could victual his castles from ships. Flint, Rhuddlan and Aberystwyth were all in the first contract. In most cases, like Flint, the scheme envisaged a strong concentric citadel attached to a walled town which was laid out on a geometrical grid plan. The town was for colonists attracted by adventure, favourable taxation laws and other inducements. The townspeople served the garrison and the garrison defended the town. It was a basic colonial solution adopted by both Edward and Saint Louis in the French Wars.

Flint was begun in 1277, a square castle with four corner towers, one of which was much larger than the others and was detached from the curtain wall so that it acted as a defensible keep. In some respects it was similar to the donjon at the Château de Coucy, built half a century earlier, massive and impressive. However, it had a strange feature, for there appear to have been two concentric walls leaving a circular central space not directly accessible to a peripheral gallery above it, so that anyone breaking into the tower might reach the central room but could not easily attack the defenders in the gallery.

Right
Caernarvon Castle from the river

John Speed's map of the town and castle at Caernarvon, 1610

Rhuddlan Castle was begun in the same year and work continued without pause until 1282. It was built on the river so that it could be supplied from the sea, and it consisted of a high lozenge-shaped inner ward with east and west gateways at the angles of the curtains, buttressed by pairs of large drum-towers. Lower walls in the moat surrounded the outer ward, providing the advanced battlements of a concentric design. To the south-west the river covered the rear of the castle but because of the slope of the ground the outer walls are here too far forward to receive effective cover from the battlements of the inner ward.

War broke out again in 1282 and it took time for Edward to starve the Welsh into submission. He then began the systematic planting of English boroughs deep in the Welsh hinterland: Conway, Caernarvon, Denbigh, Criccieth and, in 1284, Harlech, the most impressive of all. Some, like Caernarvon and Criccieth, were adaptations of earlier Welsh castles. Most of the remaining work at Criccieth dates from its Welsh occupation, although the two drum-towers of the inner ward were strengthened and heightened by the English. Caernarvon, begun in 1283 and still unfinished by 1323, was planned as a seat of royal government and a palace for the Prince of Wales after the English abandoned the idea of using Rhuddlan as their capital in Wales. Caernarvon Castle has a strange plan. Its walls follow a long irregular contour interspersed by towers and give support to a gridiron fortified colonial town. The curtain walls are high, sometimes splayed at the base, and a crosswall originally divided what is now optimistically described as an inner and outer ward. Concentric defence, or rather, supporting fire, was provided from the battlements of the high towers and, from a curious feature, a number of additional small towers which rose even higher within the core of the main towers. Eagle Tower has three of these devices. The proportions of the octagonal towers, and the way in which stripped masonry of dark and light stones has been used, are so reminiscent of Constantinople that one must accept that the linear quality of Caernarvon is modelled on the New Rome.

Conway, with its walled town, stands on the river's edge. Also designed by James of St George, it was started in 1283, ready to receive its garrison in only two years and almost completed in five. It was very expensive, with building costs running in the region of £6,000 a year. One can appreciate the expenditure poured out by the English exchequer in this programme of holding down Wales. By 1285 Conway alone was employing 1,500 builders; it was the most costly of all Edward's castles in Wales.

Using Conway as a springboard, Edward I, in the year 1283, passed his army along the coast to Harlech. With them went masons and quarrymen for the construction of this majestic castle, for Harlech represents the summit of medieval castle-building. Perched on a craggy site, it looks out over the bay of Cardigan to the towers of Criccieth, clearly visible on the opposite shore. Its plan is symmetrical on an east-west axis. It consists of a commodious inner ward containing the main garrison accommodation and is surrounded by a high curtain wall between three and four metres thick. From the corners project circular towers with turrets, similar to those at Caernarvon, rising within the towers on the north and south fronts. The outer ward is narrow and its battlements, which follow the perimeter of the main curtain, are kept low so that the tiers of fire are closely integrated. On the east face a great bulk of masonry encases the entrance to the inner ward, and this was to become the characteristic keep-gatehouse of the English castle. The concept was not entirely new; in embryo it can be seen in the Porta Nigra at Trier and the gatehouses of Roman towns in Britain. James of St George had used it earlier at Rhuddlan and in a modified form at Caernarvon. And the idea of placing a citadel in the forefront of the attack, and yet capable of complete isolation from the remainder of the fortress, was seen at Krak des Chevaliers. But the essence of the English keep-gatehouse is in the idea of creating an active defence by pushing the headquarters into the forefront of the battle so that the commander can witness and be fully informed of the progress of the assault. His living and fighting accommodation were therefore provided in this building. In addition to one portcullis on the main gate another was probably provided at the rear of the keep-gatehouse so that it could be completely isolated from troops in the rest of the castle. This was always a useful precaution against the possibility of mutiny. Psychologically the keep-gatehouse imposes a feeling of strength at the point most vulnerable to attack and

emphasises the age-old theory of the effect of deterrence. This device appears to have worked at Harlech for in 1294 the castle was besieged by Prince Madog whose forces were repulsed by a garrison of 37 soldiers. The immense expenditure of between £8,000 and £9,000, nearly £1m. in modern money, on this one building was thereby justified.

Beaumaris Castle belongs to the third period, after the Welsh Revolt. It was begun in 1295 and the outer curtain was added in 1316 by Nicholas de Derneford, certainly carrying out St George's original design. Beaumaris is somewhat similar in plan to Harlech, although the site is very different. Low down on the shore, on a flat site, it watches the northern entrance to the Menai Straits. Because of the threat of attack both from the land and along the narrow coastal strip from the sea, Beaumaris duplicates the keep-gatehouse and additional semi-circular towers are introduced mid-way along the curtain on the east and west sides, equal in size and strength to the four corner ones. The moat originally went right round the castle and the low outer battlements were provided with flanking fire from smaller regularly placed towers. Except for the little dock, built for the safe anchorage of English ships, and the position of the northern gate, the plan has an almost perfect symmetry.

Left
Harlech Castle

Above and right
Beaumaris Castle

Right and below
Caerphilly Castle

Below right
The great barrage at Caerphilly

Caerphilly is not one of the royal castles built for the control of Wales. Lying in the south of the country, it belonged to Gilbert de Clare, ninth Earl of Gloucester, and son in law of Edward I. It took a long time to build and is therefore more complex and less articulate than Harlech and Beaumaris. Probably James of St George was involved in the work for the inner castle bears some resemblance to Beaumaris. It has an approximately square inner ward with four corner towers and a powerful keep-gatehouse on the east face capable of being cut off by portcullis from both inside and out. There is an outer battlemented ward surrounded by a moat, so the defence system was concentric. On the west side there is another keep-gatehouse which provided supporting fire for the west gate in the outer battlements, buttressed between two further drum-towers. One suggestion is that at some date the castle was turned round and the western gatehouse defences built on what became the new front; for protecting them is a further defensive system called a hornwork, with its own gateway and drawbridge spanning a further moat. The ground to the north and south was flooded to provide an impenetrable barrier some 150 metres across. In order to do this the great barrage, a triumph of engineering, was constructed across the whole eastern face of the castle, forming a front of over 250 metres. The barrage consisted of a double wall with towers and massive buttresses and, behind these, wide platforms or terrepleins for the outermost defence of the castle. It was a truly formidable concept. Although thrice attacked, on each occasion Caerphilly Castle held out.

By 1296 Edward had conquered Scotland. Wallace's revolt of the following year was cracked at Falkirk and the English began to consolidate their position by the construction of castles in a manner they were already adopting in Wales. James of St George went north in 1302 and in the following year he was probably engaged on the design of the great keep-gatehouse at Kildrummy Castle which, both in shape and scale, is not dissimilar from Harlech. The castle is now badly damaged but it seems clear that the general layout of the enceinte predates the English occupation and probably drew direct inspiration from France. The present plan is almost semi-circular with a keep-gatehouse in the centre of the semi-circle and large drum-towers at the north and west corners, the latter being more pronounced and reminiscent of the donjon at Coucy. The connection is easy to establish, for Alexander II of Scotland married Marie de Coucy in

Top left
Kildrummy Castle ; plan

Top
Bothwell Castle ; plan

Above and left
Caerlaverock Castle (Crown Copyright)

Castell Coch

1239. The similarity with the donjon tower at Bothwell Castle, also thirteenth century, is even more pronounced. Here the tower is much larger than its neighbours and is partially isolated from the inner ward by a segment of moat constructed inside the castle.

Caerlaverock Castle is the third important Scottish example dating from the thirteenth century. It links the semicircular plan of Kildrummy and the asymmetrical but pointed solution at Bothwell to form a perfect equilateral triangle with a powerful keep-gatehouse at one apex. Caerlaverock is well-preserved, its curtains and towers rising directly from the waters of the moat. This is no concentric design. It was begun in 1290 and successfully besieged by the English in 1300 who held it until 1312. The keep-gatehouse, the western curtain and the southern tower date from the period of the original castle. The eastern tower and the other curtains are mainly fourteenth century and perhaps the evidence is too scant to prove that they stood upon earlier foundations, and that the castle was originally triangular.

Throughout Britain castle-building was incessant in the fourteenth and fifteenth centuries, the need for heavy fortification slowly giving way to the provision of more comfortable living accommodation.

Although an almost entirely nineteenth century structure Castell Coch, near Cardiff, is interesting for it successfully reproduces, certainly on the outside, the characteristics of an early fourteenth century Welsh castle. It was restored in 1875 with imagination and artistic licence, but with considerable integrity, by the Marquess of Bute and his architect William Burgess. It stands on a hillock and has an almost round

courtyard with circular towers on the north, east and south faces. The entrance gate and drawbridge lead between the first two towers with the southern tower acting as a keep. The main hall and living accommodation lie between the keep and the southern or kitchen tower.

Bodiam Castle in Sussex is a fine representative example from the late fourteenth century. It was built in 1385 to defend the countryside from French naval raids, the river Rother being navigable as far as Bodiam bridge. The castle plan is rectangular with four corner drum-towers 9 metres in diameter rising to a height of over 18 metres, thus dominating the lower curtain wall which is further supported by rectangular towers in the middle of three sides and an elaborate keep-gatehouse on the fourth. The castle stands in a wide moat and was approached by narrow bridges and a walkway which swung at right angles in front of the keep-gatehouse in

order to expose the unshielded sides of attackers in true classical manner.

In France the tradition of castle-building goes back earlier than in Britain. The Franks had carried their ideas with them to the Holy Land and embodied them in the castles of the crusaders. Swabian kings had taken them to Italy and the Normans brought their tradition to England and later to Scotland. In France there still stand the innumerable remains of castles and fortified towns dating from the eleventh century onwards.

Carcassonne is the finest remaining example of a town defended by concentric walls of fortifications but has been elaborately restored by Viollet-le-Duc. The core of the inner rampart dates back to the fifth century and was erected by Visigoths. Outside this lies an open passage, or esplanade, some eight metres wide and then the outer rampart, battlemented and lower. The ground, clear of scrub and trees, drops away so that the city stands on a clearly defined natural plateau. Round, square and semi-circular towers with turret roofs project from both curtain walls at regular intervals. There are only two gates to the city, guarded by drawbridge, portcullis and bartizan, and the defence is strengthened by a high-walled citadel.

Aigues-Mortes is also thirteenth century. It was laid out by Louis IX in 1240 on the Rhône delta to form a base camp for troops embarking on the crusade. The town is approximately rectangular in plan, with streets crossing at right-angles. It has a high curtain wall punctuated at regular intervals by towers which rise above the ramparts of the curtain and are topped by additional slender turrets like

Carcassonne ; plan

Below left
The high concentric walls of Carcasonne

Bottom left
*Walkway between the inner and outer
walls of Carcassonne*

Below
The citadel at Carcassonne

Military Architecture

The Tower of Constance at Aigues-Mortes

The walls of Aigues-Mortes

Château-Gaillard; plan

The donjon at Loches

those found at Caernarvon. Where the streets terminate at the town walls the towers are coupled in Roman fashion to accommodate additional garrisons at these vulnerable points. At one corner stands the massive Tower of Constance, a typical French donjon, built between 1241 and 1250 as a safe residence for the king. Isolated from the town walls, which are in any case later in date, it is an almost solid chunk of masonry pierced by very thin arrow slits and with two fine gothic vaulted rooms some 12 metres high scooped out of its interior. The present battlements date from the seventeenth century. The walls of the town were constructed after Louis' death in 1270 by his son Philip the Bold and carried out by a Genoese contractor called Boccanegra. Their splendid preservation is largely due to the fact that the town lay on the deserted sandhills of the river delta.

Loches has one of the most impressive donjons in France. The castle was begun soon after 987 by the Comte d'Anjou as part of a policy to place fortresses at strategic points in order to consolidate his conquests in Touraine. Like most early designs the donjon is rectangular. Constructed of rubble masonry with an inner and outer dressing of cut stones, it rises to an awe inspiring height of 37 metres. Its sides are now flanked by tall slender semi-circular buttresses which were added towards the end of the eleventh century. They appear to provide little additional strength to the mighty keep, but perhaps they did if their dressed masonry penetrated deeply into the rubble wall. In the twelfth century Loches was in the hands of the English who built the main enceinte. In the following century three beautiful and strangely shaped towers, each formed like an almond, were attached to stiffen the defence.

Right
Château de Coucy; after Viollet-le-Duc

Far right
The château at Josselin

Below right
Drum-towers of the château at Angers

Château-Gaillard was built by Richard Cœur de Lion in his French domain. It stands ruined on a finger of land rising from precipitous cliffs 90 metres above a bend on the river Seine. Begun in 1196 when the traditional square and rectangular keeps of the French castles like Langeais and Beaugency were being replaced by polygonal or circular ones, Château-Gaillard displayed the latest techniques in military architecture. Probably it was partly designed by Richard, who knew the crusader castles, for there are similarities with Saône. The castle consists of a V-shaped forward bailey on the edge of the spur, separated by ditch and drawbridge from the middle bailey which forms the outer fortification of a concentric design supported by the vastly thick segmentally buttressed walls of the inner bailey, and the steeply battered and buttressed walls of the great circular keep or donjon.

In 1203 it was attacked by the French and surrendered after a bitter siege; an unusual circumstance for so powerful a fortress in an age when castles could be considered impregnable. But the attack was both painstaking and audacious. All the traditional tools of the besieger were utilised, including siege-towers, battering-rams, scaling-ladders and ballistae. Every type of projectile available was thrown at the walls of the castle, supplies were cut off and the garrison were starving. Four hundred women and children were sent out from the walls but the French, acting correctly within the rules of war, refused to accept these refugees who spent a miserable winter sandwiched between the opposing lines and so reduced by starvation that having eaten the dogs they consumed their own children. In the spring, missile engines and sappers resumed the attack, a tower collapsed from mining and the French captured the middle bailey. The English were now bottled up in the inner bailey and the strong donjon. Eventually, the walls fractured by mines and shattered by catapults, a breech was made sufficiently large to allow the French troops to pour in for the final attack and the garrison surrendered.

Farther south the château at Angers was unsurpassed in its expression of power and self-sufficiency. Seventeen large drum-towers, splayed out at their base, were built along the curtain of St Louis' castle between the years 1228 and 1238. They must once have looked even more daunting, for before the Wars of Religion they rose two storeys higher dressed by machicolations and pepper-pot roofs. The whole concept is a remembrance of the past for, although more closely spaced, the drum-towers are strongly reminiscent of Roman usage in such places as Portchester.

The castle at Coucy was destroyed by the Germans in the First World War, but it is known from drawings and engravings and is important because of the great influence it exerted on later building. It was constructed between 1225 and 1240 on the edge of a high cliff 46 metres above the valley of the Aisne. Here the French abandoned the concentric system of defence for a castle of enceinte with powerful curtains, depending for their defence upon even more powerful circular flanking towers. The upper castle, an irregular quadrilateral with corner towers, had as its core a great circular donjon 32 metres in diameter with walls 7·5 metres thick at the base, completely surrounded by its own moat which isolated it from the rest of the castle. Inside it had three rooms, one above another, each vaulted from a central column; the structure stood over 60 metres high.

Josselin in Brittany is the epitome of the French medieval

Left
Pierrefonds; after Viollet-le-Duc

Below left
Mombeltrán; from Alberto Weissmüller

Right
Medina del Campo; from Alberto Weissmüller

castle. Three of its nine giant cylindrical towers rise from the rocky banks of the river, savage and awesome. Once they were topped by a chemin de ronde from which projectiles could be dropped upon anyone foolish enough to attack the base of the castle. This projecting gallery originally continued along the top of the curtain wall making it higher than it is at present. The main structure on the south-west river façade is late fourteenth century.

Pierrefonds near Compiègne in northern France has been much altered in the restoration by Viollet-le-Duc, but the main walls and towers and the general external appearance are a faithful restoration of what once existed. In spite of the liberties taken in the restoration of the interior and the outworks the castle gives a remarkably true impression of what such a fortress must have looked like at the height of its power. It was begun towards the end of the fourteenth century and completed early in the following century, one of a group of castles acquired or constructed by the Comte de Valois to form a vast military area threatening Paris. It was eventually restored under the personal initiative of Napoleon III, that remarkable ruler with a flair for architectural aggrandisement. Viollet began work in 1857 and when criticised about the far-reaching nature of his restoration called it 'a fine lesson in popular history'. The plan forms an irregular parallelogram perched high on a commanding site. It combined the provision of ample luxurious apartments with the need for security. Thick walls, regular towers, the double system of concentric defence and the ability to pass troops rapidly from point to point so as to be able to reinforce any menaced position were all incorporated. Tiers of machicolations on the towers and the curtain walls provided four stages of defence one above the other.

In Spain war raged up and down the peninsula for centuries as the christians tried to expel the Arabs. The reconquest began in 718 but it took some 200 years to reach the Douro river, a distance of only 130 miles. It was not until 1492 with the surrender of Granada that the Arabs were finally expelled. There was also a struggle within a struggle, for the unification of Leon and Castile with Aragon, when christian fought christian. Most of the great castles lie in Castile and differ from those in France and England, for feudalism was never so strongly entrenched, and the buildings were required more for the garrisoning of troops than for the living accommodation of the lord.

Mombeltrán, near Avila in the Kingdom of Castile, probably dates from the thirteenth century; it has a square plan with concentric defences and one considerably enlarged corner tower acting as donjon, similar to Flint and Bothwell.

La Mota at Medina del Campo is a large well-preserved brick castle, trapezoidal in plan, with part of the central core of its concentric defences dating from the thirteenth century and the rest of the building begun in 1440 and completed about 1479. From this last period dates the great square tower which rises to more than twice the height of the inner curtain wall of the battlemented and towered outer enceinte. By the time this part was built cannon and handguns were in regular use and gunloops were provided all along the battlements in passages on two floors.

In the province of Segovia, Coca is also late, built in the fifteenth century by the Archbishop of Seville as a giant castle-palace. It is a sort of brick caricature of Harlech, but less symmetrical as the keep-gatehouse is replaced by a traditional corner keep representing a castle in miniature. Everything is over-exaggerated, the talus, used at Krak, now occupies most of the surface of the outer walls and towers, and the battlements drip rich Arab *mudéjar* decoration. There are gunports for heavy cannon, some placed three feet above the floor of the dry moat and others facing out from above the line of the talus in the thick curtain walls and the hexagonal corner towers. Altogether one gets the impression that Coca was designed for its effect rather than for its efficiency under siege conditions.

In Italy can be traced a gradual regression in military effectiveness from the powerful modelling of Frederick's Norman castles to the florid exuberant manifestations in late medieval castles like Sirmione. Little wonder that these last card-like structures fell apart so disastrously under the impact of explosive-powered cannon at the end of the fifteenth century. It was the Italians too, realising the deficiences of their late medieval castles, who were the first to carry out major reformation in the art of fortification throughout the first half of the sixteenth century. In the interim the Italian peninsula, like other parts of Europe, bristled with castles too numerous to cover in any detail. A selection will illustrate some of the main characteristics.

The tower at Bitonto built about 1384 is a plain free-standing drum 16 metres in diameter and 24 metres high. There were once many in this area of Apulia. In character it seems to have come straight from the Norman fortresses. Gaunt and forbidding, thick-walled and powerful, it is as though a corner tower of Frederick's castle at Catania had been detached to stand ground on its own.

Lucera, built between 1263 and 1283, is still the great medieval castle of enceinte. Almost rectangular in plan it stands high on a spur looking out over the plain of Foggia and is separated from the town by a deep ditch. The castle has a great courtyard enclosed within a curtain wall, punctuated at close intervals by powerful rectangular towers. The land-front facing the ditch has seven sharp-angled towers spaced between the drum-towers which act as pivots to the eastern and western corners of the fortress.

Towered walls at Lucera enclosed a fortress, but towns too needed to be defended and the enceinte system was also applied to them. In the thirteenth century there were many walled towns in Italy, though most have now been pulled down or replaced by later fortifications. Montagnana near Padua still has its complete circuit of walls with a circum-ference of over a mile. These were probably begun by Ezzelino il Monaco shortly after he captured the town in 1242 and were continued until his death in 1256. By that time the high square towers of the Castello San Zeno, which supported the town walls and acted as a citadel, had been completed in stone. Work on improvement and restoration continued for another century and probably much of the present city walls dates from 1360; they were designed by Franceschin de Schici.

Monteriggioni near Siena is Montagnana in miniature. Built in the thirteenth century its complete circuit of curtain wall punctuated by square towers at regular intervals encircles a small hilltop town. It was mentioned by Dante in the *Inferno*. Nearby San Gimignano is also walled but its defensive character is emphasised by innumerable em-

The towers of San Gimignano

Below left
*Rectangular towers on the east front of
Lucera Castle*

Below
*The walled town of Monteriggioni near
Siena*

Bottom
*The town walls and the Castello di S Zeno
at Montagnana*

battled towers rising like diminutive skyscrapers and giving the town a unique flavour. In the fourteenth century when most of these towers were built to protect their owners against civil strife and display an arrogant expression of power there were already many such towers in central Italy. Bologna once had clusters of these tall thin rectangular towers, although only three famous ones now remain.

The Este Castle at Ferrara is typical of fourteenth century Italian military architecture. Built to provide palatial accommodation for a rich noble family, it was constructed on a square plan surrounding a central courtyard and approached through four battlemented gateways guarded by portcullis and drawbridge. Its corners are reinforced by square towers the lower courses of which splay out to give additional strength and thickness at foundation level and at

Opposite
The fortified dock at Sirmione

Entrance to the Este Castle at Ferrara

the same time make attack across the enveloping moat a hazardous undertaking. The curtain walls and the towers are topped with traditional Italian machicolation composed of corbelled brick ribs projecting from the vertical surface of the wall and joined by semi-circular arches. Behind these lie the holes through which boiling oil and other combustibles could be dropped on assailants. The upper storeys of the walls and towers are later additions.

Characteristic of all these Italian castles, which in their hundreds still dot the countryside, are high walls topped by elaborate machicolations and stiffened by rectangular or square towers. Most towns in the north have their examples. The once forbidding exterior of the castello at Mantua has been weakened by the introduction of later windows and the pantile roofs which cover the jagged edges of the fifteenth century machicolations. Sirmione, which stands on a spit of land jutting into the waters of Lake Garda, is a splendid example of the late medieval phase. It is a brick castle and was built by the Scagilieri in the fifteenth century. The waters of the lake are channelled to form an effective moat and it even has its own dock surrounded by a crenelated defensive wall. Its walls and towers are extremely high and although thick and strong they give all the appearance of having been cut from cardboard.

By the middle of the fifteenth century many of the Italian military engineers resorted again to the use of the round drum-tower as a better means for deflecting projectiles, especially with the threat of the explosive cannon. The Castello Orsini at Bracciano north of Rome was begun in 1470 and completed in 15 years. It has an irregular pentagonal plan with two main courtyards and its walls are

stiffened by means of cylindrical towers. Its walls and towers, however, are still high, menacing in appearance but vulnerable to bombardment. The round tower of the fortress at Roveretto built in 1488 was also very tall, but it gained a degree of security from its almost impregnable site.

Gradually the engineers began to appreciate the advantages of lowering the profile and rounding the edges of the new fortresses so as to present a minimum target to a besieger's artillery. Early attempts to offset the effect of cannon fire, both by the introduction of counter-batteries and the reduction in height of castle buildings, are to be found in the work of the last decades of the fifteenth century in the Romagna, the Marche and Lazio. Strength still depended on mass, gunports were few and small, and round drum-towers were immensely broad, often being steeply splayed out towards their bases from string courses sometimes more than halfway up their total height. The round towers consequently left large areas of dead ground which could not be covered from the small gunports.

Imola (1472–73) has this immensely stolid appearance, but probably the rocca at Senigalia built about 1480 was the most classic expression of this type of fortress. It has a low squat symmetrical form, square, with massive corner drum-towers whose scale is emphasised by the close spacing of the ribs in the machicolations: the base of the towers was still intended to be protected by these devices. The towers and the curtain wall rise to the same height and form a continuous solid platform for the defending artillery. Forli (1481–83) is similar but it still retains the traditional keep or mastio abutting one wall of its quadrangular plan. At Sarzana near

The Castello Orsini (Odescalchi) at Bracciano

La Spezia both the town bastion and the fort built by the Florentines in 1487 follow this pattern.

Already gunpowder was seen to be affecting the medieval castles of Italy, but before discussing its full significance, there are other areas of Europe which require passing reference. In north-western Europe there are many fine examples of castles and fortified towns still well-preserved.

's Gravensteen at Ghent

Vulnerable Belgium, lying in the path of powerful armies, is full of strong castles but probably the most powerful is the castle of the Counts of Flanders, 's Gravensteen at Ghent. It was begun in its present form in 1180 by Philip of Alsace who had seen service in the Holy Land and well knew the crusader castles of Syria. The keep, which is Philip's work, is a large thick-walled rectangular structure braced externally with buttresses and with walls which are in places 1·7 metres thick. It stands in the middle of an elliptical enceinte which rises from the waters of the moat, strengthened by 24 turrets constructed like buttresses.

The banks of the Rhine, which has always been the most strongly fortified river in Europe, are studded with castles and fortifications. They present a varied picture as each German state tended to develop its own characteristics. Some, like Elts on the Moselle, display a continuous process of building from the twelfth to the sixteenth centuries.

Farther to the north-east the golden age of the Hohenstaufen monarchy is displayed in the Imperial Castle at Nürnberg. It was a rich complex of buildings originating from the tall round Sinweh Tower built about 1200. At first this stronghold of the Holy Roman Empire protected the town, a mere huddle of houses which clustered around the base of the powerful castle, but later as in so many European towns the position was reversed and the strongwalled town succoured the castle which was gradually relegated to the task of acting as a citadel. The town of Nürnberg was encircled by a double bank of strong fortified walls punctuated and reinforced with powerful drum-towers so that its concentric system of defence could deter any attack. Early in the fifteenth century during the Hussite Wars the fortifications

Left
The Imperial Castle at Nürnberg; plan

The Sinweh Tower in the Imperial Castle at Nürnberg

on the north and west sides were strengthened and the Imperial Castle was incorporated into the town's defences. The programme of improving and strengthening the defences was continued into the sixteenth century when the burghers availed themselves of the latest Italian techniques and employed an Italian military engineer, Antoni Fazuni Maltese, to lay out imposing bastions in the Italian manner between 1538 and 1545.

Some medieval walled towns still stand intact. Dinkelsbühl has a complete circuit of walls, four fortified gates and some 18 additional tall thin towers placed at intervals straddling the town's walls. Rothenburg on the Tauber is similarly defended. The town's walls and towers date from the thirteenth and fourteenth centuries with additions like the Spitaltor, a strong circular sixteenth century bastion, designed for artillery and containing two oval inner courtyards. Built in 1572, Rothenburg remains to this day a typical sixteenth century German fortified town.

The square castle with four corner drum-towers has always been one of the most simple, direct and effective defensive statements. From the castles of Frederick in Sicily, to Edward I's great castle at Harlech, to fourteenth century Bodiam and fifteenth century Imola and Senigalia, to sixteenth century Civitavecchia, this plan form persisted and became, with the substitution of triangular bastions for drum-towers, one of the most popular solutions to fortress design. L'Aquila in the sixteenth century and the innumerable colonial forts constructed in the seventeenth and eighteenth centuries are typical examples. It was a well-tried solution which has since withstood the test of time.

Muiden Castle in Holland is of this progeny. The original

Far left
The Grüner Turm at Dinkelsbühl

Above and left
The Pulver Turm at Rothenburg on the Tauber

65

The Muiderslot

castle was built in 1285 so that the square plan with round corner towers is close in date to Harlech, but there is no concentric system. In 1386 the castle was rebuilt on its original foundations. It was restored between 1895 and 1948. The building is in brick and is surrounded, like all fortifications in Holland, by water defences. The curtain walls are high but the corner towers are considerably higher, topped by steep-pitched conical roofs. The square gatehouse in the centre of one curtain is approached over the moat by a bridge. The main living accommodation lies on the far side of a generous courtyard, its roofs rising at ridge level higher than the battlements of the adjoining towers.

RENAISSANCE FORTIFICATIONS

The medieval world perfected a type of defence which was normally resistant to direct attack. Height and thickness of wall were vital for a small garrison to hold off a large invading force. This was the supreme age of the castle, whose invulnerability was to collapse before the onslaught of gunpowder, mining and powder-operated cannon. Here is the great change which signals the Renaissance and one of the major problems whose solution taxed its greatest thinkers.

The two basic testing grounds were against the English castles in Normandy at the end of the Hundred Years War and against the Italian castles in the invasion of Charles VIII in 1494. But already by the end of the fourteenth century the impact of gunpowder was having its effect on the theory of warfare. The defence was still vertical, the utilisation of high walls being imperative because of the vast investment in existing castles, but walls were also thickened to withstand impact. Even new ones depended upon thickness for their strength. The curtain of Salses Castle in southern France was 18 metres thick. Exposed walls were sometimes covered with timber or earth to resist the shock of cannon balls. Circular or rectangular towers tended to be replaced by pentagonal or oblique-sided ones, to deflect shot. Combustible timber projections were removed from battlements

and the ditch made more of an obstacle, wider and deeper so that a breached wall would not fill it and make a bridge for the attackers. Nevertheless, the balance of power was slowly shifting back to the attacker.

Much of the changed pattern can be attributed to the northern Europeans and the French. Charles VII employed two brilliant brothers, John and Gaspar Bureau, to reform his artillery and introduce innovations. In this field the most important modification was the substitution of cast-iron for stone shot. The calibre and consequently the size and weight of guns was reduced to fire the mass-produced and more accurate cast shot. The resulting gain in penetration led to a tremendous increase in the number of guns used. The new French artillery with these advantages took the field against the English in 1449 and, for the reconquest of Normandy, was involved in 60 sieges in a period of one year. Whereas the English had taken a month in 1415 and four months in 1440 to conquer Harfleur, Charles's army recovered it in the depth of winter in only 17 days. Often the mere sight of artillery was sufficient to cause a town to capitulate.

Trunnions were cast into the guns and made sufficiently strong for them to carry the weight and bear the shock of discharge. This meant that the guns could actually travel on their firing carriages and could be brought into action quickly. One of the features of the invasion of Italy in 1494 was the way the French guns could be used to support infantry in the initial stages of an assault, instead of following miles behind and only slowly being brought into action. Fast horses which could keep pace with the rest of the army replaced oxen to draw gun carriages. The fortresses collapsed under the fury of the French guns and mortars, and the highly efficient French artillery proved its superiority at Agnadello. At the battle of Ravenna in 1512 and at Marignano three years later its employment decided the issue of the day. Probably the first writer to appreciate the full import of the new weapon was a woman, Christina da Pizzano, whose military treatise, the most complete work on the art of war since Roman times, was completed about 1410. Daughter of an Italian professor invited to France by Charles V, she must have been one of the most extraordinary women of her age. She read widely but was discerning and capable of penetrating analysis so that her work remained a valuable source of reference in western Europe throughout the fifteenth century, being translated into English in 1488.

The second potent instrument was the explosive mine. It is not known when it was first used. Possibly it was employed by the brothers Bureau, but Taccola has been credited with its invention and he shows a drawing of a powder mine in his *De Machinus Libri X*, completed by the mid-fifteenth century. It is known that during Gonsalvo of Cordova's siege of Naples in 1495 his engineer, Peter of Navarre, exploded a mine under the walls of the Castel Nuovo much to the astonishment of the garrison. In 1501 another mine was exploded at the siege of Cephalonia.

From the fourteenth century onwards the art of war and fortification became a popular subject for study. Many of the early treatises were from Germany where there was already a profound interest in firearms. Konrad Kyeser's *Bellifortis*, dedicated in 1405, traces the growth of the new technology of war. In addition to the usual siege engines handed down from Roman times and slowly perfected, Kyeser shows a wheeled artillery chariot mounting 14 guns and protected by projecting scythes designed to cut to pieces any infantry that approached too near. Also illustrated are an armoured car to shelter sappers and soldiers and a rotating cannon consisting of six barrels which fired in turn: by the end of the century some of these machines were in use. In 1397 the Della Scala family were operating three large chariots, each of which carried 144 small mortars mounted in three tiers, a formidable weapon. Kyeser shows a wide interest in military engineering, formulating proposals for boats propelled by paddle wheels, a kind of landing craft with tailboards which could be lowered to allow the disembarkation of infantry, and telescopic bridges which could be winched out across a river by means of cables.

Guido da Vigevano's treatise, written about 1335, was a guidebook for the king of France to take with him on a crusade, a manual on hygiene and medicine, with 13 chapters on military machines that were likely to be useful in sieges in the Holy Land. The age is full of works demonstrating methods designed to overcome the obstacles of the defended castle or town: plans for bridges that can be thrown out across ditches, vehicles that can travel like submarines along the bed of a river or ditch, boats to be navigated without vulnerable oars, and vehicles which can be self-propelled.

The art of prefabrication, for rapid movement and erection, was already carried to a considerable degree of finesse.

By the mid-fifteenth century, that is even before the shattering invasion by Charles's efficient French army, the Italians were doing much of the investigation into the art of attack and defence. Many of the investigators were theorists and humanists, not practising soldiers and engineers. Tartaglia noted that 'the eye of the mind sees more deeply into general things, than does the eye of the body in particulars'. Each author drew on and plagiarised the work of his predecessors. Roberto Valturio, typical of this age, was commissioned by Sigismondo Malatesta to write *De re militari libri X* which was completed about 1460. Some of its drawings were copied from earlier works. Alberti was a humanist and he admitted in his *De re aedificatoria* written about the same time that he was not a military man. Only a small part of his treatise is about defence and then only because he was interested in the design of cities. His main source was Vegetius, but Alberti expressed some thoughts of his own. He outlined the need for flank defence between towers 'so that whoever offers to approach between the towers is exposed to be taken in flank and slain; and thus the wall is defended by these towers, and the towers mutually one by another. The towers should have an open gorge at the back so that, if captured, they cannot be used against the besieged'. Alberti seems hardly to have considered the implications of attack by gunpowder except to acknowledge that the ditch is the most formidable method of defence. He thus underlined a problem which was to tax the minds of military men for generations to come: should the ditch be filled with water or should it be kept dry?

The city should have a citadel, the last point of defence for its ruler and its garrison and counterpart of the medieval keep-donjon, capable of being held against subversion and treachery. The ruler must always fear treachery and for this reason the building should be 'bugged'. Pipes were to be secretly concealed in the walls so that the conversation of strangers and servants could be heard. Among other forms, Alberti advocated the star-shaped citadel which was to become an accepted solution by the beginning of the sixteenth century. Understanding the nature of greed, he stated 'neither public bodies nor private persons can ever set bounds to their insatiable desire of getting and possessing still more and more; from which one source arises all the mischiefs of war'. On the value of fortification as a deterrent he observed 'It ought to look fierce, terrible, rugged, dangerous and unconquerable.' Perhaps this belief caused him to conclude that victories could be gained 'more by the art and skill of the architect, than by the conduct or fortune of the generals'.

Machiavelli's ideas have been much misrepresented but because of his important diplomatic position and his clarity of thinking his *Dialogues on the Art of War* are important. In general Machiavelli came out against dependence on fortresses and in favour of an efficient citizen's army. He advocated the value of earthworks and field fortifications to support his army. He realised and expressed the dilemma of his age: 'If the walls are made high they are too much subject to the blows of artillery; if they be made low they be most easy to scale'. He placed much reliance on ditches, but feared that those outside city walls might be filled by attackers. Therefore he advocated broad deep ditches inside the enceinte, an expedient adopted in the defence of Padua in 1509 when a continuous ditch was dug inside the rampart flanked by small casemates just as Machiavelli had recommended. But the device was normally only employed as an expedient to retrench a breach in the walls by a ditch hastily excavated immediately behind the breach, as at Mendz in 1552 and Siena three years later.

Antonio Averlino, called Il Filarete, proposed a new city for Duke Sforza of Milan, the description of which was contained in a treatise completed in 1464. The city had of course to be defended but Filarete broke little new ground, his military ideas being based firmly in the past. He gave precise instructions on the dimensions for building walls, towers and gates, but clearly his interest was more in the symbol of the ducal castle than in its power to resist an assault. However its outline is interesting for, inscribed within a circle, the walls were arranged as a tenaille fortification, like the teeth of a saw, an idea reintroduced by Montalembert in the 1770s.

Emerging as the most important military engineer at the end of the fifteenth century was Francesco di Giorgio, for he combined practice and theory, architecture and engineering. Between 1480 and 1486, his most fertile period, he was living and working at Urbino where he designed and built a ring of fortresses on the hilltops protecting the approaches to the city. Francesco's treatise on civil and military architecture was completed about 1480, the first major work on the art of fortification in the modern world. He was convinced that the strength of a fortress depended upon the quality of its plan rather than the thickness of its walls and he therefore became preoccupied with the trace. Like Filarete he advocated the tenaille system of serrated walls and carried his

ideas into effect at the Rocca di Mondavio, at Cagli and Montefeltro, all of which were illustrated in his treatise. The outline of his forts varied, often being triangular, but most were influenced by the belief he still held in the need for a strong central tower as a point of safety in the last retreat. Francesco di Giorgio appears to be one of the first engineers to use the caponier, a loopholed room where the defenders, protected by masonry, could fire along the floor of the ditch or indeed any other flat vulnerable surface in the fort.

The rocca at Mondavio was built between 1482 and 1492 and shows that, however advanced Francesco di Giorgio's ideas on military architecture may have been, in practice he was forced to be conservative and still stuck to the medieval concept of a high stronghold or keep as the ultimate defence in a threefold system of an entrance tower isolated by drawbridges, a support tower and a four-storey keep. There is no courtyard and every inch of space is used. The only precaution that was taken against damaging blows from cannon balls was to slope the walls in the form of an escarpment from a line two-thirds of the height up the tower. This was a device which also made scaling more difficult.

The concepts of war were changing and its prosecution becoming much more a matter of specialisation. Textbooks written for soldiers by soldiers now became a feature of the times. One of the most outstanding was by Philippe Duc de Cleves. In 1498 he wrote *Description de la forme et la manière de conduire le faict de la guerre*. As commander of the French army and governor of Genoa he was fully conversant with the tactics and strategy of his time and he showed how the professional soldier was becoming increasingly aware of the importance of geography and climate, of a need for thorough

Top
Plan of the fortifications of Sforzinda by
Filarete

Above
Two forts; from Francesco di Giorgio,
Trattati di Architettura

*Reconstruction of a fifteenth century breech-loading
gun firing through an embrasure at Mondavio*

knowledge of the topography of the site for a siege, and the importance of reliable information gained through reconnaissance. As the conduct of war moved into an area of specialisation, the military engineer, versed with a thorough understanding of mathematics, thus came to the aid of the soldier. Thus Alberti could write that 'the besieged . . . would inform you that their greatest defence lay in the art and assistance of the architect'.

The two outstanding geniuses of the age were Leonardo da Vinci and Dürer. Outstanding because although they inherited a knowledge of the past they were able to think clearly about the conditions of the day and in particular about the profound effect on any defended position of accurate and heavy fire from cannon and mortars. Leonardo thought of himself first and foremost as a military engineer; painting and sculpture were only sidelines. About 1483 he offered his services to Duke Ludovico Maria Sforza, claiming the invention of portable bridges which were indestructible, a knowledge of how to besiege and destroy any stronghold, a method of transporting mortars which could throw stones like a storm and make smoke which could cause terror amongst the defenders, and the ability to cut mines, even under rivers and trenches, without making a noise. Concern-

ing his knowledge of unassailable, irresistible chariots he wrote: 'And behind these, infantry would be able to follow quite unharmed and unhindered'. It is known now that much of this technology was drawn from other sources, in particular Valturio. However it is in the design of fortifications that Leonardo made his most revolutionary proposals. The characteristic of medieval fortifications had been the use of high though comparatively thin curtain walls which in addition to being vulnerable to enemy bombardment provided inadequate platforms for the efficient utilisation of the defenders' artillery. Although, aided by the force of gravity, height was useful for dropping objects on to assault troops assembled at the foot of the walls, it had the disadvantage of causing the defenders' artillery to use plunging fire. If this did not hit on first impact, it caused the cannon ball to bounce high and its effect to be wasted. Like his fellow engineers in the fifteenth century Leonardo advocated making the defence walls lower and more sturdy to resist the enormously increased power of artillery. His machines, tanks, rapid-firing guns, the use of a type of shrapnel and breach-loading mechanism, were all part of the theory if not the practice of his day. His drawings in the *Codice Atlantico* made at the end of the fifteenth century show the development of a ravelin not only to cover the gate, the weakest point in a curtain wall, but made sufficiently large so that the face of the ravelin is grazed by flanking fire from the two adjoining towers of the main wall. Leonardo described it thus: 'The ravelin, shield of the fortress, should be defended by the fortress, as the fortress is by it'.

Already engineers were approaching the solution of the bastion which will be discussed more fully later. Even the flanks of round towers were pierced by embrasures so that guns in the casemates could enfilade the curtain and the crown of the parapet. In 1502 Leonardo was made engineer-general to Cesare Borgia's forces in the Romagna and became concerned with the problem of minimising damage caused by projectiles hitting the curtain wall of a fortress. Exposed surfaces were made elliptical, slanting back as far as possible. Leonardo became preoccupied with the profile of the reveals of the gun embrasures, asking 'why a ball hitting a wall obliquely does not go through, as when it hits at right angles'. There followed a study of pointed projectiles using aero-dynamic fins. Leonardo replaced battlements with a massive cupola elliptically shaped to deflect shot. He provided three tiers of casemates to greatly increase fire power and built-in smoke vents to clear their interiors, always a problem until the introduction of smokeless powder in the nineteenth century.

Hung on the face of his forts he used grass or hay soaked in water in order to deaden the impact of shot. Francesco di Giorgio's caponiers were by now fully developed circular ones, approached by underground staircases and placed at the angles of a fortress to survey and protect the vulnerable bed of the ditch. In Leonardo's final drawings he brought

Left
*Design for a fortress; after Leonardo da
Vinci*

Below left
*Studies of enfilading artillery fire in front of
a ravelin; after Leonardo da Vinci*

*Design of a fortress showing arcs of fire;
after Leonardo da Vinci*

together many ideas in a complete synthesis of defensive techniques. A quadrilateral fortress depended upon line behind line of casemated gun positions, low, with their top faces splayed towards the enemy in a continuous shallow line. Each ring of defence, separated by a ditch from the one in front, was a continuous gun platform: a fortress thus conceived was an active element in war. In this form he had achieved a balanced defensive position, each part reciprocally protected by its neighbour, with low profiles and the minimum of exposed surfaces. It was a defence in depth with detached works pushed forward mutually protectable by flanking fire.

The Fort de Salses, built in 1498 by the Spanish engineer Ramiro Lopez to defend the approaches to Roussillon, shows that it was not only the Italians who were acutely aware of the damaging effect of artillery fire on permanent fortifications. Salses was designed in the form of a square with corner drum-towers and a powerful high keep in the centre of one wall, so far a traditional concept. Like the Italians Lopez adopted the idea of steeply scarping the walls of the drum-towers, in this case from about half way up their total height, a device which had been used in early medieval times to stiffen defence against battering-rams and which found renewed popularity in the roccas of fifteenth century Italy. But the significant features of Salses which foreshadowed later developments were the low-lying profile of the fort in general, its buildings sunk into a deep wide ditch, the curved upper surfaces of the curtain walls designed to deflect shot, the use of large gunports for heavy artillery to cover the ditch, and the provision of detached outworks formed like semi-circular ravelins in the ditches.

Albrecht Dürer in his *Instructions for the Fortification of Cities* carries a study of the casemate further. In his proposals circular artillery towers would flank a city wall and have casemates low down to give grazing fire in the ditch, some 60 metres wide. His casemate walls were hollowed out to allow the guns to run forward far enough for their muzzles to project beyond the embrasures and so keep down the smoke inside. One metre diameter smoke flues were carefully designed to keep the internal atmosphere clear. Durer's projects were vast in scale, involving expensive masonry, with the result that his treatise, published at Nürnberg in 1527, tended to be overlooked for several generations, his ideas being superseded by those of the Italian engineers of the sixteenth century and not revived until many generations later.

As theory was put into practice siege warfare became once more gradually stabilised and commanders realised that the guns which had so effectively reduced a stronghold could equally well be used for its defence. Artillery duels from carefully sited gun positions, with bombardment scientifically applied, became from this time on the main feature of the siege. Nicolo Tartaglia, a mathematician from Brescia, produced in 1537 his *Nova scientia* the first important treatise on the scientific application of gunnery and the first attempt to evaluate the trajectory of shot.

The greatest step forward in the techniques of defence was the introduction of the bastion. The use of towers to provide mutual defence and to flank an intervening curtain wall goes back to ancient times, but the principle had been applied in a haphazard manner. Both square and round towers left areas of their surface which could not be covered by fire from their neighbours. Engineers now discovered that by introducing triangular bastions, with batteries of guns protected and concealed in their flanks, it was possible if they were properly sited to ensure effective enfilade fire across both faces of a bastion from the flanks of its two adjoining bastions. The length of the line of defence, from the salient of the bastion to the guns in the flank, was dependent upon the effective range of those guns. No attacking troops could penetrate to the face of the bastions or their intervening curtains without passing through a barrage of fire, and it was realised that enfilade fire was far more effective than direct fire from guns firing forward which might miss assaulting infantry.

The invention of the bastion was undoubtedly Italian and it looks as though, with the early development of field fortifications by the Italians, its origins must be sought in that province rather than in permanent stone fortifications. Field fortifications lend themselves to experiment, but with so much of the evidence destroyed it is almost impossible to attribute to any one man the invention of this or that feature in the development of fortification. Certainly earthwork bastions were used at Ravenna in 1512 and Verona in 1516, and Della Valle in his *Libro continente appertentie ad capitanii* (1524) advocates as a practical soldier the use of bastions because they are more quickly built than walls and less susceptible to artillery fire. About 1461 Michele Canale had constructed the Bastion Verde to reinforce the defence of Turin but the shape of his work has been obscured beneath later works built by the French after 1536. Francesco di Giorgio made drawings of embryonic bastions and by the time of the Sangalli's work in central Italy this had become

*Reconstruction of the rocca at Ostia by
Giovanni Montiroli; after Guglielmotti*

common practice so that the claim that Sanmicheli was the first to use it on the Bastione della Maddalena at Verona in 1527 is clearly unsubstantiated. This was Vasari's claim, but it appears that this bastion was designed by Michele dei Leoni and added to by Sanmicheli after 1530. It has been suggested that Pierre d'Aubusson, superintendent of fortifications for the Knights of St John in Rhodes from 1472 and Grand Master there from 1476 to 1503, was the first to introduce the bastion in substantial form in a series of works which culminated in the Boulevard d'Auvergne in 1496, but these knights' towers seem much closer to the four-sided pointed towers which the Romans sometimes attached to their curtain walls, and are unrelated to the systematic employment of enfilade fire in a co-ordinated defence.

The second step was to extend the defence in depth. To some extent the new bastion did this, but gradually additional works were pushed forward to reinforce the front and hold off an enemy at a distance. The covered way became a platform outside the ditch where troops could carry out a forward defence. Tartaglia has been credited with this invention when he also advocated that the counterscarp should be made as high as possible in order to shield all the internal fortifications below the breastworks. However, a type of covered way was probably used in the fortifications of Brescia in 1428. New structures behind the magistral line, which marked the crest of the main fortifications, also deepened the field of defence. Cavaliers, great bulky blocks, rose behind the bastions and sometimes behind the curtains, standing up like cavalrymen so that their guns had a clear view of the countryside beyond the glacis.

The Italian Wars threw up a number of competent practitioners who had gained experience in the fierce sieges of many a central Italian town. Hilltop fortresses were constructed at first with bulky round towers whose surfaces, and those of the curtains, were steeply scarped to deflect shot and to ensure that an enemy using scaling ladders would have to prop them at a dangerously oblique angle. Baccio Pontelli's work on the rocca or fort at Ostia (1483–86) belongs to this period. Ostia is important because it is probably the first example of a Renaissance building designed exclusively as a fortress and not as a palace or a residential castle. Pontelli worked with Francesco Giamberti, but was strongly influenced by Francesco di Giorgio. The appearance of the rocca was largely medieval for it has a triangular plan with three drum-towers at its points. The strongest rises higher and acts like the medieval mastio. It was surrounded by a pentagonal bastion, one of the most interesting contributions to the plan, scooped out with casemates for artillery and disposed so that its guns could at least enfilade one curtain wall and support an adjoining tower. The fort at Civitavecchia also dates from this period. It is a rather conservative fort, rectangular in shape, with four corner circular towers and a projecting seven-sided keep or mastio designed by the architect Bramante, the middle of the northern face being completed by Michelangelo.

During the first two decades of the sixteenth century there was feverish fortress-building when theories were put into practice and, so long as results were being observed, there was little new theorising. The Sangallo family of architects and engineers had a major hand in the work in Italy which was to dominate the European scene for a century. From

Above and right
The Fortezza di Firmafede at Sarzanello

The mastio of the fortezza at Civita Castellana

1500 until the rise of the French school, itself dominated by Vauban, the Italians held the field with their new bastioned system of defence, nearly all major fortifications being carried out by them. Francesco Giamberti was the eldest of the Sangalli, designer of the forts at Sarzana and Sarzanello.

For a short while the triangular fort became popular. It was used as far away as Scotland at Caerlaverock Castle and found several expressions in fifteenth century Italy. Its chief disadvantage was the narrowness of the fighting area at the points of the triangle. Sarzanello was originally a triangular fort with its vulnerable entrance in the middle of one curtain covered, slightly later, by a detached triangular ravelin so that the overall perimeter of the building assumed the shape of a bisected diamond. The walls of the drum-towers, the curtains and the ravelin are scarped towards their base from a string course two-thirds of the way up their exterior surfaces. Although on a hilltop, the fortress has a comparatively low-lying profile and is sunk into an encircling dry ditch. The towers and the ravelin do not rise above the parapet of the curtain walls, so that the whole fortress appears flat-topped with the exception of its traditional square mastio which rises higher in the centre of the fort. Giuliano da Sangallo was responsible for many other works of military architecture including Colle Val d'Elsa (1479), Poggio Imperiale (1488) and defences at Arezzo and Pisa.

His eldest son, Giuliano da Sangallo (1445?–1516), was also an architect and a sculptor. With Baccio Pontelli (1450–92) he designed the triangular fortress at Ostia (1482–86). This is similar to designs made by Francesco di Giorgio, who was probably referring to Pontelli when he mentioned in his *trattato* that another architect had stolen some of his

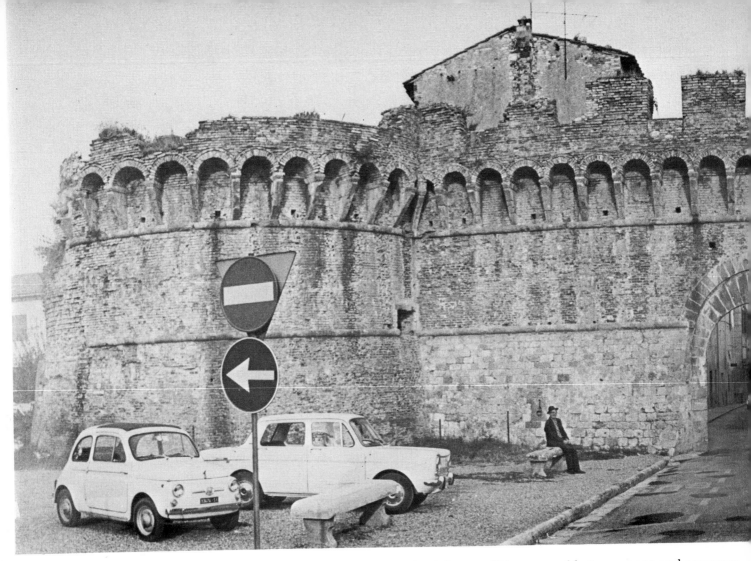

inventions. Giuliano was an active military engineer engaged in a number of sieges and he directed the attack on the fort at Sarzana designed by his father.

His brother, Antonio da Sangallo the elder (1455–1534), was responsible for some of the most important transitional fortresses in Italy. In 1493 he modernised Castel Sant Angelo in Rome by substituting triangular bastions for the old circular drums. At Civita Castellana (1494–97) Antonio da Sangallo designed a palace-fortress for Cesare Borgia, pentagonal in plan with two circular and three triangular bastions whose battlements lie level with the parapet of the curtain. The traditional central mastio was retained, octagonal in shape and rising higher than the rest of the fort. The design of his fort in Nepi built about 1484 is traditional, consisting of a rectangular plan with corner circular towers. In 1499 he be-

gan the defences of Livorno and between 1501 and 1502 was building his most important design, the rocca at Nettuno. This last is one of the most interesting and well-preserved forts in Italy showing the emergence of the full bastion plan. It was quite detached from the walled town, although later an outer town enceinte was added which joined a corner of the fort, so Antonio had considerable freedom of action. He conceived the building as a perfect solution to both the practical and theoretical problems. It was square in plan, in line with the neo-platonic ideas of his time, and had four identical corner bastions whose faces were correctly aligned with the line of defence from the flank of the opposite bastion. The shoulders of the bastions were rounded to become embryonic orillons. Because of the talus of the curtain walls there was no room for batteries low down in the flank but

Above
*The Porta di Volterra at
Colle Val d'Elsa*

Forte del Sangallo at Nettuno

only at parapet level. The mastio was retained and rose high above the curtain on the seafront façade.

The fort (1508–15) at Civitavecchia was retrograde for it had round towers. Its basic plan is like Nepi but with Bramante's mastio projecting beyond the curtain on the north façade. Antonio's villa-fortress of Caprarola begun in 1515 and completed by other architects is described later.

Antonio da Sangallo the younger (1483–1546), nephew of the elder Antonio, carried the Italian bastion design to its logical conclusion. He became the acknowledged expert on Italian fortifications, his great opportunity opening as a result of the shake-up of defences following the sack of Rome in 1527. The younger Sangallo designed the fully bastioned enceinte around the port of Civitavecchia. During the siege of Florence he was opposed to Michelangelo's defensive system and was later commissioned to remodel the town defences and to build the Fortezza da Basso (1534). This fort shows the full transition to the Italian bastion system. A contemporary writer, Baccile da Castilione, stated that 'the best praise that can be given to him who designed it is that it has never been used as a fort in war; but only as a symbol of power'. The angle bastion was fully established as the standard solution to the problem of the defence of towns. Vasari described it: 'the defence work enjoys a reputation all over the world and is believed to be impregnable'. One should remember that it was designed as much for internal security as external defence.

Rome's deficiencies had been cruelly demonstrated in the sack of the city, and Antonio was called during 1537 to work until his death on the vast programme for the defence of the Vatican outlined by Paul III. Machiavelli advised and Michelangelo was involved, along with numerous other engineers including Jacopo Castriotto.

The so-called Forte Michelangelo at Civitavecchia with (left) *the town walls; after Fer, 1697*

Design for fortifications; after Michelangelo

Project for the Porta al Prato at Florence; after Michelangelo

Below
*Plan of the dei Riformati Bastion at
Verona by Sanmicheli*

Michelangelo (1475–1564) was engaged on two major projects of fortification. In 1529 he was procurator-general for the defence of Florence and from 1547 to 1548 was engaged on the work of rebuilding the Vatican fortifications. It is not known whether the sketches which remain were fanciful scribblings or actual projects for earthworks which he so strongly advocated. The Florentine defences, mainly outworks, are now destroyed. Surviving drawings, probably depicting temporary defences to buttress the walls of Florence and made about 1528, show a remarkable vitality and a complete change from the passive concept of defence to a dynamic aggressiveness. The forms of his bastions take on an organic appearance, unrestrained by the strict geometry which is such a feature of the regular work of the Italian school. Michelangelo's drawings are difficult to decipher, but the baroque curves were primarily intended to deflect shot. The weakness of his design arose in the restricted field of fire through the limited aperture of the embrasures and the need therefore for a multitude of defensive artillery. Ackerman has brilliantly described his designs as follows: 'His bastions spring from the walls like crustacean monsters eager to crush the enemy in their claws'.

Michelangelo's contribution to the costly work of fortifying the Vatican was problematic but from Vasari it is known that he was involved in a monumental row with Antonio da Sangallo the younger. Sangallo, who had faced him at Florence, accused him of being a sculptor and a painter but not a military engineer. To this he replied that he knew little of those arts, 'but of fortifications, considering the thought he had devoted to it over so long a time, and his practical experience, he believed he knew more than Sangallo and his whole family put together'.

Michele Sanmicheli (1484–1559) was the other great Italian practitioner of the first half of the sixteenth century. His opportunity came in 1530 when he was commissioned to complete the ring of fortifications which would safeguard Verona, a strategically placed city on the plain facing the route from northern Europe through the Brenner Pass. His bastions, which embraced the west and south sides of the town, were smaller than later designs, having long sections of curtain wall between them. The della Trinita Bastion, the first to be completed, was obtuse-angled in plan, giving it little working depth for the manhandling of guns. Consequently, in his later designs he tended to make the salient more acute. The shoulders of his flanks were square and the flanks themselves joined the curtains at right angles. The flank of each bastion contained a *piazza bassa*, a casemate for

The Porta Nuova at Verona

Façade of the Porta Nuova at Verona; after Ronzani-Luciolli

Plan of the fort of S Andrea, at Venice

artillery low down to cover the ditch and enfilade the curtain.

Two of Sanmicheli's gates still stand well-preserved at Verona, although their abutments have been cut away to allow modern traffic to circulate. The Porta Nuova (1533–40) lies in the middle of the curtain protected by two bastions. However the gate, in addition to its architectural embellishment and rusticated masonry intended to give it the appearance of strength, was also designed as a cavalier. Its top surface was provided with gun embrasures and strong parapets capable of making it a defensible position; it was in fact the earliest known artillery-defended gateway. By about 1550 Sanmicheli had changed his approach, for the Porta Palio, although equally impressive on the outside, was a less strong device, incapable of supporting heavy artillery on its roof and dependent upon its adjoining bastions for defence.

In 1534 Sanmicheli was requested to report on the defence of Venice, and subsequently he constructed his classic fortress at the entrance to the harbour, Sant Andrea on the Lido. This, plus a line of ancillary forts, was to protect the seaward approaches, with land fortresses in strong points such as Treviso, Padua, Vicenza and Verona ringing the landward approach.

Sanmicheli was one of the last of those artists whose work embraced a variety of disciplines. Brunelleschi, Bramante, Michelangelo, Leonardo and Benvenuto Cellini were all able to combine the practice of military architecture with other pursuits, and Sanmicheli's civil architecture is at least as important as his military undertakings. For the next generation of Italians the complexity of the subject called for specialisation and there emerged the highly skilled and independent profession of the military engineer.

Stokesay Castle

From the time of the downfall of the Roman empire life in the country had been hazardous and it was as a result rarely populated by men of means. Only the castle or fortified town was safe from predatory raids or armed invasions. In fact the Mediterranean littoral remained susceptible to the marauding attacks of corsairs well into the middle of the eighteenth century. However in some places conditions improved, with stable government and some relaxation from the need to maintain high standards of defensive architecture. There emerged the semi-fortified villa, conceived partly as an aristocratic symbol.

In Britain Stokesay Castle (1240–1305) shows how a fortified manor house could already, at the end of the thirteenth century, provide a reasonable level of comfortable accommodation. The hall is spacious, nearly 16 metres long and some 10 metres high, providing sufficient space for the lord's family, his guests and his servants. Set aside between the hall and the south towers is a solar, a room open to the sun's rays, with a pleasant view across the wooded countryside and providing some measure of privacy and comfort for the lord and his family. Two peepholes were cut through the party walls so that he could keep an eye on guests and retainers in the hall below.

Hurstmonceux Castle (1441) is a vast brick structure built upon a square plan with bold salient octagonal towers and an impressive gateway. It was not designed to be put to the test of a siege but to symbolise the martial traditions of an arrogant ruling class. It is 'a magnificent parade of browbeating feudal pride'. Lulworth Castle in Dorset still shows four large drum-towers at the corners of a rectangular plan, but the curtain wall is adorned with richly decorated Renaissance doors and windows, no bar to a violent intruder.

Above
Hurstmonceux Castle

Lulworth Castle

Alberti, in his *della famiglia* written about 1432, was the first to revive the idea of the villa. Quoting from Roman sources he extolled the qualities of a life in the country, not too far distant from a place of work in the city. From the time of the early Renaissance there sprung up, first in Italy and then elsewhere, buildings which retained a semblance of the fortified character of their predecessors. There is an almost imperceptible change from the castle with palatial accommodation to the palace containing an element of defence, at first functional but later only symbolic and romantic.

The French were no less proud of their chivalric background, and a group of châteaux on the Loire were built in the sixteenth century which show the change from fortress to house. Langeais (1465–70) still presents a formidable exterior, but the garden façade is already gentler. Chaumont still retains the massive circular corner towers, its walls are machicolated and its gate is covered by a drawbridge, but both the towers and the curtain walls are pierced by commodious windows. Chambord has a quadrangular plan with massive drum-towers, but the walls are pierced by large areas of glass and the skyline cluttered with delicate decoration which would topple at the first discharge of a cannon. The Bohier wing at Chenonceaux (1515–22) and Azay-le-Rideau (1518–27) are either wholly or partially surrounded by water, but although the architecture contained elements of castellated design they were never intended to withstand assault.

The lower stages of the Villa Farnese at Caprarola were modelled on the pentagonal plan of a fortress with five angled bastions, but the superstructure, mainly designed by

Above
Langeais

Left
Chenonceaux, showing the Bohier wing on the right

Above right and right
Azay-le-Rideau

Following page
The Verdala Palace in Malta

The Palazzo Farnese at Caprarola; after Ferrerio and Falda

The Palazzo Farnese at Caprarola; after Ferrerio and Falda

Vignola between 1559 and 1573, was a stately high Renaissance palace. Not so Verdala Palace in Malta (1586) designed by Gerolamo Cassar; even at this late date the building retains an element of defence, although the windows are quite large. There was a ditch and loopholes in the flanks of the small bastions for musketry defence. It was necessary for the grand master in his summer residence to take precautions against a commando-like attack by the Turks.

Unlike the semi-fortified villa, the Scottish tower houses of the sixteenth century did not utilise defensive devices for purely symbolic reasons. These buildings were primarily houses designed for private living, safeguarded against the ever-present threat of sudden attack. They were high narrow buildings, cleverly designed so that their plans conformed to the shape of a Z or an L. Thus by staggering the towers so that overlapping fields of fire could be poured from the wide-mouthed gunports on the ground floor, an all-round ground defence could be maintained with minimum expenditure on a few handguns. As circular rooms do not provide the most convenient spaces for living accommodation, the upper rooms of these houses were cleverly turned into rectangular spaces by corbelling from the round tower. Claypots, near Dundee, built on the Z plan between 1569 and 1588, is a splendid example of this type of house.

In the mid-sixteenth century Britain once again resorted to the construction of important fortified works to defend her coast. The peaceful years of the preceding reign had helped fill the coffers so vital to Henry VIII to fit out a British field

Claypots (Crown Copyright)

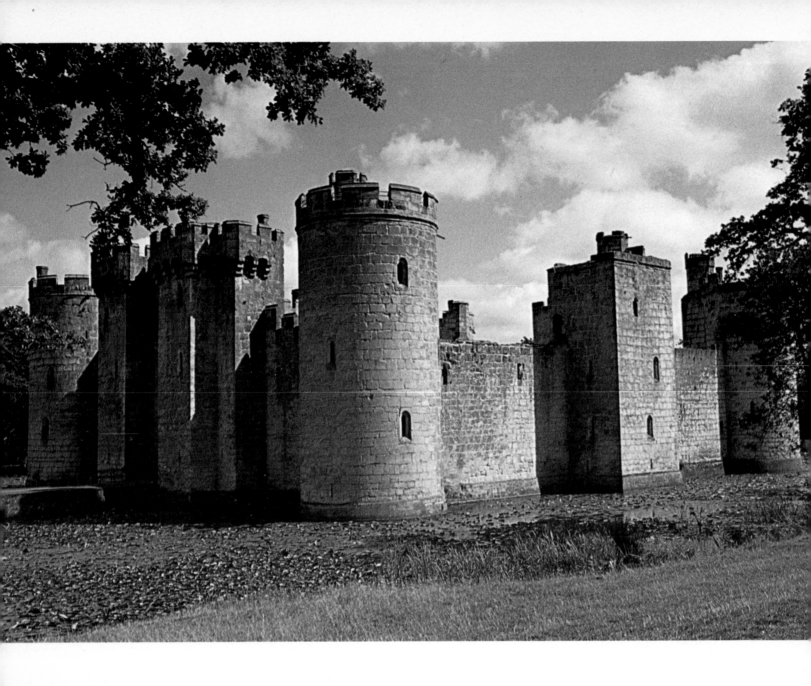

Bodiam Castle (photo Lawrence Edwards)

army for service in Europe. The expeditionary forces of 1513 and 1523 may have made little impact upon the European scene but they certainly provided the English king with an opportunity to make contact with European practice in the art of fortification and gave him a lifelong fascination for artillery. For many years the practice of fortification in Britain had dwindled into insignificance and the revolutionary systems of the Italian engineers seemed no more than distant rumours. It is therefore understandable that when Britain came once more to re-arm her standards of fortification should be rudimentary. Henry VIII's exchequer had been buttressed from the spoils gained through the confiscation of church property, so he undertook the most expensive scheme of coastal defence that Britain had ever witnessed. Along the south coast, at vulnerable points facing France, new forts were erected on a scale quite unprecedented. They stretched from the mouth of the Medway to the great bay at Milford Haven. Three of the most interesting examples, known as 'the castles which keep the downs', lie close together. Deal, Walmer and Sandown were all built between 1539 and 1540 to protect the anchorage which lay within the Goodwin Sands. They were pure forts rather than castles, designed as powerful artillery platforms and were probably the work of Stephen von Haschenperg, a German military engineer employed by Henry between 1539 and 1543. All the forts were centrally planned, with rounded bastions mounting tiers of guns both in casemates and on barbette platforms. The forts invariably had a higher round central keep and were encircled by ditches. There was nothing elsewhere at that date quite like them.

Certainly they were a long way from current Italian practice, but Dürer, who was advising on the defences at Antwerp in 1520, designed semi-circular bastions with sloping parapets and there were other examples in north-eastern Europe from which von Haschenperg's ideas may have sprung. The German engineer was sacked in 1543, officially for bad behaviour and extravagance, but perhaps because Henry already had a shrewd idea that the engineer's knowledge was not up to date. However before he left he had designed Sandgate, probably St Mawes and the central fort at Pendennis, whose outer italianate bastion was added in 1598. Pendennis was started in 1539 and St Mawes in the spring of 1540. Both were finished by 1543. Dover had a low-lying shore battery added to its defences. The fort at Camber was constructed on a site which had in the past repeatedly attracted French landings. There were four new forts on the Hampshire coast, supplementary work at Portsmouth and numerous other defences stretching away to the west.

Britain braced herself for an invasion likely to be mounted under the pretext of the divorce of Catherine of Aragon. An opportunity was further provided by the truce between Francis I of France and the Emperor Charles V of Spain reinforced by the Pope's bull of excommunication and the preaching of the crusade against Henry. In 1539, 1,400 men were digging and building on the Downs defences and the work was rushed forward. But invasion never came and, except against isolated raids, the forts were never put to the test, perhaps fortunately for although adequate against any naval bombardment of the time most would have found it difficult to withstand a landward assault.

Work was also undertaken to strengthen the last English foothold in France. John Rogers (†1558) and Sir Richard

Deal Castle; aerial view and plan

Above left
*A contemporary cannon; a 12 pounder
brass basilick cast in 1554 and presented to
Henry VIII*

Top right
St Mawes

Right
Pendennis Castle

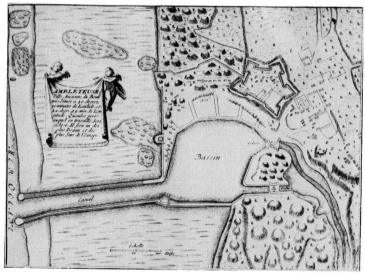

Lee (?1513–75) were the two English military engineers engaged in the work. Contemporary drawings are valuable for illustrating the rapid transformation which took place in English fortress design between 1541 and 1546. In those years, under the pressure of war and the brilliant endeavours of a powerful king, Britain rapidly hoisted herself, in the art of fortification, from a medieval situation to a position where she could at least claim some parity with her European neighbours. Rogers's early essays at Guines Castle near Calais and in the perimeter north of the Humber near Hull are primitive expedients modelled on the forts Henry was constructing along the coasts of Britain. At Guines Rogers developed the quatrefoil-shaped bastions into pointed trefoils pushed forward, with flanks from which guns could enfilade the curtain walls. The shapes are certainly unusual although there is precedent in eastern Europe, and Francesco di Giorgio many years earlier tentatively sketched in a similar proposal for a bastion. The snag was that portions of dead ground in front of the bastions could not be covered by protective fire, and guns firing from the flanks along the face of their adjoining curtains would probably have hit the flanks of adjoining bastions. In the fortress at Ambleteuse and in the fortifications around Boulogne Rogers adopted the Italian triangular-shaped bastion as a measure of defence against enemy cannon fire. The transformation seems so sudden and so complete, in a matter of three or four years, that one must suspect the assistance of some Italian engineer. Henry VIII had a part to play, for he was a king with strong ideas who overruled Rogers's design for a triangular fort at Ambleteuse, preferring his own pentagonal scheme. At Boulogne the king added primitive cavaliers behind Rogers's bastions and inserted a radial city plan for the town, an idea which could only have come from Italy itself or from Italian designers working abroad. Rogers's lack of experience may have been crucial and could account for his eclipse as an important military engineer after Henry's death in 1547. This eclipse was not necessarily caused by the vindictiveness of his enemies. More likely he was found wanting, too set in his ways to cope with the rapid changes in the art of fortification which spread across the Channel. Neither can he escape some censure for the rapidity with which the British fortresses in France crumbled against the onslaught of the French armies in 1557. He paid the price, dying as a prisoner of war in French hands in the following year.

Sir Richard Lee, the first English architect to be knighted, had been with the army in Calais. In 1545 he was ordered to survey Tynemouth Castle where already there were Italian engineers working with the British. To Tynemouth he took two experts, Antonio da Bergamo and Giovanni Tomaso Scala. In 1557 Lee was in the Netherlands, and in January of the following year he was appointed to survey and strengthen the fortifications of the border town of Berwick-on-Tweed, which was to become his most important undertaking and the most serious British exercise in fortified town design to have survived. Lee shortened the medieval circuit of walls and threw a girdle of Elizabethan ramparts across the north and eastern faces of the city, its curtain walls and bastions modelled on the early Italian school of fortification. The work was remarkably advanced, equal to anything carried out elsewhere. This was particularly true of the Cumberland and Windmill Bastions, with their obtuse-angled plans, their flat-headed orillions and their *piazze bassi*, all of which were very close to Francesco Laparelli's work on the landfront at Valletta in Malta (1566). It is remarkable that an English engineer should have so quickly grasped the essentials of the Italian system, though it was less surprising that Elizabeth should have commissioned him, knowing her distrust of foreigners and in particular Italians. But Lee was only one of a number of men who were critically examining the new art of fortification. Paul Ive was amongst them. His *The Practice of Fortification*, printed in 1589, was one of the earliest English books on the subject and although it drew heavily on Italian and French sources showed a penetrating mind and a man with practical experience.

Shocked by the loss of Calais in 1558 Queen Elizabeth strengthened the defences of her kingdom. Berwick was only one aspect of the work. Between 1570 and 1577 Ive was working on the Castle Cornet in Guernsey where he carried out the first stage of enveloping the old medieval fortress within a protective sheath of Tudor fortifications. The second stage, built between 1593 and 1597, clothed the whole front with Italian bastions. In 1598 Ive was working at Pendennis on a similar outer screen which proved strong enough to withstand a five months' siege by Fairfax's parliamentary army in 1646, one of the stoutest resistances of the Civil War. An almost identical enceinte was constructed by Federico Giannibelli around the medieval castle at Carisbrooke in the Isle of Wight, built mainly between 1597 and 1600.

Portsmouth was the only fully defended town in southern England. King's Bastion and the long curtain on the waterfront are part of its original fortifications dating from the fourteenth century, and Southsea Castle was built nearby in 1544 as part of Henry VIII's policy of strengthening the coast. Even in Henry's reign the town was encircled by walls on the landward side strengthened by circular towers and fully developed Italian triangular bastions to the north-east. But the main task of providing an effective bastion trace fell to Bernard de Gomme in the middle of the seventeenth century. De Gomme began work in 1665 to provide an integrated defensive system of bastions and ravelins and their supporting works which will be described later.

THE BAROQUE WORLD: DEFENCE IN DEPTH

Chapter four

The 1550s saw an avalanche of publications on the theories of military architecture in Italy. Various hypotheses were tested in battle by experts who gradually developed a specialised knowledge in their field. An extraordinary consistency of style emerged which can be described as the later Italian style of fortification probably brought about by the fact that nearly all those who wrote were practitioners whose exclusive province was military engineering. Except on rare occasions defensive systems no longer formed part of general treatises on architecture and the military engineer emerged as a professional man in his own right.

The system utilised the triangular bastion projecting beyond the main curtain-walled defence. At first bastions were very small and curtain walls very long so that guns on adjacent bastions had difficulty in flanking one another, that is providing effective enfilade fire across the face of their neighbour bastions. The ditch, 30 to 40 metres wide, had a counterscarp approximately parallel to the faces of the bastion so that this counterscarp formed a zigzag pattern on the outside of the defences. After about 1540 a covered way, a protected passage for infantry so that they could move around screened from the fire of the attackers by higher ground, was added to the Italian system. The first recorded use of the covered way was at Brescia in 1428. However the details of its construction are not clear and Tartaglia is often credited with the invention of this feature which was in regular use after 1540.

During the sixteenth century the Italians improved their construction and spread their ideas throughout Europe. Almost every sovereign state employed them and in Spain and the Low Countries they had ample opportunities to build and test new fortresses.

The ideal solution was constructed upon an interior polygon, although often in practice the engineers had to use their ingenuity to defend irregular sites or to modify earlier defensive systems.

The ideal front, the distance measured from the points of two bastions, was between 250 and 300 metres. The faces of the bastions were arranged so that they formed a prolongation of a line drawn approximately from the gun positions in the flanks of their neighbouring bastions. These flanks projected at right angles from their curtain walls and so formed an obtuse angle with the face of the bastion. The curtain wall, which has always been the most vulnerable part of the defences was, in the early stages, covered by a semi-circular ravelin. Later in the Italian system it was covered by a tri-

Top
Two solutions to a typical bastion of the Italian school; after Zastrow

Pietro Cataneo's design for an ideal city

angular one, formed like a broad arrow with its faces some 60 to 75 metres long, standing as an isolated outwork in the middle of the ditch. The intention was to force an enemy, before he penetrated the curtain wall of a town or fort, first to attack and capture the ravelin only to find himself still isolated in the middle of the ditch. He would next have had to direct his attack against one of the bastions only to find that this was protected on whichever side he attacked by an adjoining bastion. All this manoeuvre had to be successfully completed before an enemy could penetrate the interior.

After the covered way had been adopted for the use of infantry on the outside of the ditch, Girolamo Cataneo proposed the re-entering place-of-arms. This was a space left at the re-entrant angles of the zigzag pattern made by the counterscarp of the ditch sufficient for the assembly of troops and munitions to be used against an initial attack or to be formed up for a sortie against a besieger's lines. This feature dates from 1567. Beyond the covered way lay the glacis, sloping ground cleared of all obstacles, buildings and trees so that the defenders had an unobstructed view of the surrounding countryside and the attackers were forced to expose themselves to view or to use the ponderous method of mining and sapping as they slowly worked their way up to the outworks of the defended position.

Many writers described these features in this period. There is room here to refer only to a few.

Pietro Cataneo is one of the exceptions to the rule that specialisation had overtaken the writers of treatises, for he devoted one book in his *I quatro primi libri di architettura*, published in Venice in 1554, to the discussion of fortification. He clearly stated the case for the Italian system. 'In view of the new weapons such as artillery, it is much more practicable to have them (the bastions) with an angular outline instead of a circular one so that every part can be much more easily defended. Each curtain can be covered by embrasures in the bastions at the corners.' He then cited a variety of solutions to the problem, his first being a perfect square with four corner bastions like contemporary examples such as the castle at L'Aquila designed by Pedro Luis Scrivà in 1535. The art of defence was becoming a mathematical science as the dimensions of each part under every variation of circumstance was calculated and indicated.

Giacomo Lanteri wrote two important works. His first, *Due dialoghi . . . del modo di desegnare le piante delle fortezze* came out in 1557 and two years later he published his *Due libri del modo di fare le fortificazione*. In these the art of fortification be-

gan to be fully served by the rules of geometry and took on the aspect of the science of mathematics. Engineers when writing treatises were usually concerned with the provision of permanent stone fortifications, but Lanteri was one of the first to introduce the subject of earth fortifications. He was born in Brescia and became chief engineer to Philip II of Spain.

There was a constant interchange of ideas amongst engineers in the field and in their published writings, and it is possible to trace the thread of ideas back to Roman theoreticians. Girolamo Maggi fought against the Turks and in 1564 brought out a publication incorporating Iacomo Castriotto's *Della fortificazione delle città*. This work was later to influence Vauban. Maggi is always credited with the introduction of the cremaillère, but Francesco di Giorgio had used a some-

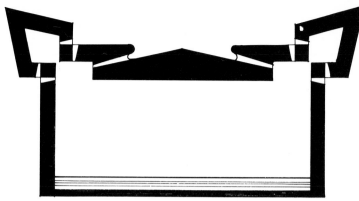

Right
The fortress at Capua; plan

Below
*A pentagonal fortress showing arcs of fire;
after de Marchi*

A fortified seaport; after de Marchi

what similar though less scientifically worked out device years earlier and Scrivà had advocated it in his design for the fortress at Capua in the 1530s. The idea was to increase the permissible length of defence by indenting the curtain wall to form a series of additional flanks from which guns could fire across its face. Maggi's and Castriotto's treatise is illustrated with innumerable clear drawings, many of them in the form of aerial perspectives. Whilst working for the Venetians Maggi is reputed to have put into operation a number of his inventions including a method of setting fire to the Turkish lines of circumvallation at Famagusta, so perhaps it is not surprising that soon after his capture by them in 1571 he should have been quietly strangled in his prison at Constantinople.

Girolamo Cataneo was a Novarese engineer who was employed on the fortifications of Sabionetta by Vespasiano Gonzaga. In 1564 at Brescia he published *Opera nuoua di fortificare, offendere et difendere*, one of the most complete treatises on military architecture. This was only the first of some half a dozen long books he wrote on the subject, spreading his reputation throughout western Europe. His works are thorough and detailed and he ranged from the broadest principles to minute details of building construction.

Captain Francesco de Marchi, an engineer from Bologna, wrote his military treatise *Architettura militare* about 1565 but it was not published until 1599. It is a most comprehensive book dealing with every sort of topic from the siting of fortresses under various conditions to the usual references to how the Greeks and Romans dealt with their problems (almost invariably added to treatises in order to give them respectability) to detailed discussions on the qualities of water. It is illustrated with a large number of clear drawings in which the author has shown the lines of fire of his defending guns and the detailed arrangements of streets and squares in a number of ideal cities enclosed within his systems of fortification. In addition to the traditional system of Italian-bastioned fortification, de Marchi, like Castriotto about the same time, illustrated the idea of completely isolating the bastions from the enceinte so that they stood, similar to ravelins, as detached works in the ditch. This disposition had the advantage of slowing an attacker by interposing an additional ditch after he had taken possession of a bastion. In a number of examples de Marchi attached the orillion, a sort of curved shoulder, to the angle between the face and the flank of the bastion. In this way the flanks were retired or set back so that guns there were partially protected by the projecting orillion. Orillions soon became common practice in fortification.

Francesco Laparelli, colleague of Michelangelo and an engineer employed by the Pope on the defences of the Vatican, did not publish his treatise on architecture, but his ideas have survived in a manuscript still in the possession of his descendants. Laparelli's description of the methods of fortifying a city, of the performance of building materials and the use and availability of labour are particularly interesting as one of his commissions, the fortification of Valletta in Malta (1566), still survives intact. Laparelli's ideas were not particularly original but he had clearly read all the sources and discussed the implications with his fellow engineers and this knowledge, coupled with years of practical experience, made the uninhibited comments in his diary of the utmost im-

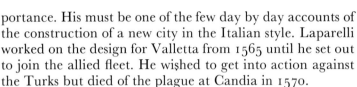

Above
Outline of a fortress; after Galeasso Alghisi

portance. His must be one of the few day by day accounts of the construction of a new city in the Italian style. Laparelli worked on the design for Valletta from 1565 until he set out to join the allied fleet. He wished to get into action against the Turks but died of the plague at Candia in 1570.

In that year Galasso Alghisi, who came from Carpi and was appointed architect to Alfonso II, Duke of Ferrara, published in Venice *Delle fortificationi libri tre*, the most beautifully illustrated treatise of the period containing sharp precise drawings. Book One was largely a criticism of the works of others, particularly those of Castriotto and Maggi. However his own designs were not without defects. Alghisi attempted to solve defensive problems by using a combination of bastions and tenailles. The tenaille is a serrated wall rather like the teeth of a saw. It was a device recommended by some German engineers but soon lost popularity in practice until it was revived in the eighteenth century by Montalembert. In Alghisi's design the trace was indented to form the tenaille, the extremities of which were capped by a bastion. In each flank of the bastion, and partly covered by the orillions, he placed a hexagonal casemate for two tiers of guns, and between each pair of casemates there was a rectangular cavalier raised to survey the surrounding countryside and to provide additional fire power. The defect of the system lay in the fact that having so pulled back his curtain walls to provide the tenaille, he left very little usable space inside the fortress.

Vincenzo Scamozzi wrote the last important Italian architectural treatise to contain instructions on fortification. *L'Idea dell'architettura universale* was published in Venice in 1615 and the second book of the first part is devoted to military

architecture. In 1593 Scamozzi had been involved in working out the design of the ideal fortified city of Palmanova for the Venetian Republic, so his theory was conditioned by practical experience. His writings are more valuable as an illustration of contemporary practice than as a source of new ideas.

It would be wrong to isolate the work of these writers without mentioning that there were many others whose books were as important and as influential as those described, men like Lorini, Belucci, Sardi and de Zanchi. Nor would it be fair to suggest that the Italians were the only ones to express their ideas on the theories of fortification during the sixteenth century. In Germany Daniele Speckle published *Architectura von Vestungen* in 1589 and was involved in the practice of his art at Ingolstadt, Ulm, Colmar and Strasbourg. He proposed several methods of fortification. His first recommended increasing the size of the bastions, which was generally done later, and providing them with triple flanks, protected by orillions, one above another for additional fire power.

He provided additional fire power on the vertical face from cavaliers which stood above the bastions and behind the middle of each short curtain. In another recommendation he furnished powerful ravelins in the ditch strengthened by flanks and a central cavalier. He also realised the importance of a covered way as one of the most essential outworks and was probably the first engineer to design this as a cremaillère, a zigzag pattern which provided numerous faces from which the defenders could fire.

French authors like Veroil de la Treille, whose *Manière de fortifier les villes et châteaux* was published in 1557, followed the Italian system. Errard de Bar-le-Duc was a more original

Within the engraving the following text appears:

d' otto lati con   tutto le sue parti.

affese reali

Disegno della meta della Forcezze

Profillo delle parti di fuori, e   di dentro à Canto alla Cortina.

Vinc Scamozzi Arch

Above left
Alghisi's proposed trace for a fortress, with square cavaliers in each bastion

Above
Fortifications for an ideal city; after Vincenzo Scamozzi

Right
Daniele Speckle's design for the fortifications of a city showing several tiers within each bastion

Palmanova near Venice; after Braun and Hogenberg

thinker. In 1604 he published *La fortificatione reduicte en art et demonstrée*. He belonged to the corps of military engineers formed by Sully in 1602 and is really the first of the great school which was to emerge in France during the seventeenth and eighteenth centuries. Although he was not singular in realising the deficiency of some of the Italian and Spanish bastions whose salients were too acute (Laparelli had already pointed this out) he was the first who fixed, at 60 degrees, a minimum angle for the salient angles of the bastions and who adopted 265 metres as the maximum length of the line of defence between the points of two adjoining bastions. The greatest flaw in his system was the result of making the angle between the face of the bastion and the flank a right angle, whereas the Italians always made this obtuse so that the angle between the flank and the curtain wall could be adjusted to a right angle. Bar-le-Duc's solution, although perhaps intended to protect guns in the flank, only provided a sharp angle which could be easily splintered by enemy fire. The device was far inferior to the orillion.

All over Europe princes and their engineers hurried to put their towns and cities into a state of defence utilising the well-tried and eminently successful system advocated by the Italians against the threat of efficient artillery fire which each year became more insistent. Though most of these fortifications have been pulled down to make way for ever-expanding suburbs, fortunately there are beautiful engravings by Braun and Hogenberg in *Civitates orbis terrarum* (1572–1618), by Merian in *Topographia Gallicae* (1644) and by Fer in *Les Forces de l'Europe* (1697), together with many individual drawings and paintings of the period.

Most engineers had to adopt irregular sites, but when the opportunity arose to design on a new site in flat country they invariably chose a multi-sided regular and symmetrical enceinte. The more sides that were used the greater the number of bastions and the nearer a line of bastions approached to a straight line. This permitted the construction of obtuse-angled bastions, less vulnerable to enemy bombardment and shorter, more easily defended curtain walls. Once the shape of the perimeter had been decided, a symmetrical figure with regularly spaced bastions, it was almost inevitable that the interior arrangement of the town, its streets, building blocks and squares, should follow a regular pattern. Many modern architectural historians have suggested that the origin of this regularity in Renaissance town planning was the result of an absorption of neo-platonic theories. In fact the shape of the town was dictated by the shape of the fortifications and this was the result of practical necessity.

Palmanova, lying on the flat land north of Venice, is a splendid surviving example of a fortified town. It was probably planned by Giulio Savorgnano in 1593. Later modified, it now consists of a nine-sided figure with angle bastions from which streets run back to a square in the centre of the town. Intermediate streets run from the centre of each curtain where, in three instances, the gates are placed. Contemporary drawings tend to exaggerate the projection of the bastions. At Palmanova they are broader and more obtuse-angled than they appear in Braun and Hogenberg's engraving. Savorgnano's defensive system depended upon the bastions and their protective ditches. Subsequently lunettes and ravelins were added beyond the main ditch to cover the points of the bastions and the curtain walls.

Valletta in Malta is probably the finest remaining example of a fortified city on a peninsula. The Knights of St John, defending Malta, had emerged successful from the Great Siege by the Turks in 1565 but the imminent threat of a fresh Turkish assault overshadowed the island. In these circumstances Francesco Laparelli was called in to prepare a master plan for the new city. The point of the peninsula was defended by the damaged fortress of St Elmo. Laparelli rebuilt Fort St Elmo on its original antiquated plan because this was the easiest and quickest thing to do and because, with the construction of the new city walls, it became no more than an advanced platform unlikely to be assaulted. If the Turks were to return, Laparelli advised the knights to construct a powerful square fort on the high ground near the neck of the peninsula. The landward front of the fort was to be constructed first and, if no time allowed, this only needed to be constructed to form the basis of the main strong landfront across the peninsula. No fresh major assault took place and the city walls were built and its streets laid out according to Laparelli's plan of 1566. The landfront of Valletta is particularly interesting because, being the strongest sector, its plan followed the principles outlined by the new school of Italian military engineers. The work is superior to Laparelli's work in Rome. Owing to the shortness of the landfront in Malta he was able to trace his curtain walls in almost a straight line, thus providing obtuse-angled bastions. He was also able to place these much closer together than had been his earlier practice in Rome where, because of the length of the enceinte, the small bastions are widely spaced. The Valletta front of 1566 is a precursor of the fully developed bastioned system of defence. Behind the bastions Laparelli placed powerful cavaliers to act as raised gun platforms dominating all the ground in front of the city. The defences stand almost as he designed them, except that orillions have been added to the rectangular flanks of his bastions and the ditch has been deepened. Low counterguards were added in front of the bastions in the mid-seventeenth century when a ravelin, now demolished, was constructed to cover the main gate.

Cities were encased wherever possible with masonry walls, but early engravings show numerous examples of the use of soil defences reinforced on their exposed vertical faces by fascines, strong wattle constructions in timber and reed to prevent the erosion of soil. Later the full advantages of earth fortifications became apparent in their ability to absorb the impact of shot without being shattered, in the lack of danger from splintering and in the ease with which a breach could be repaired.

Nearly all the main towns and cities of Europe were re-fortified in the second half of the sixteenth century or at the beginning of the seventeenth century. Some, like Willemstad (1565), were new foundations. Numerous illustrated examples remain: Philipville (1555), Alkmaar (1597), Mannheim (1606), Charlesville (1608) and, in the overseas colonies, towns like Quebec (1606).

Mannheim, lying at the confluence of the Neckar and the Rhine, is an interesting example of a fortified town. The contemporary illustrations agree on the general disposition of the fortified works but not on their details or proportions. Depending on one's point of view there was a heptagonal citadel supporting or subjugating the town whose total area was scarcely larger than that of the citadel. A bridgehead

The Muiderslot at Muiden

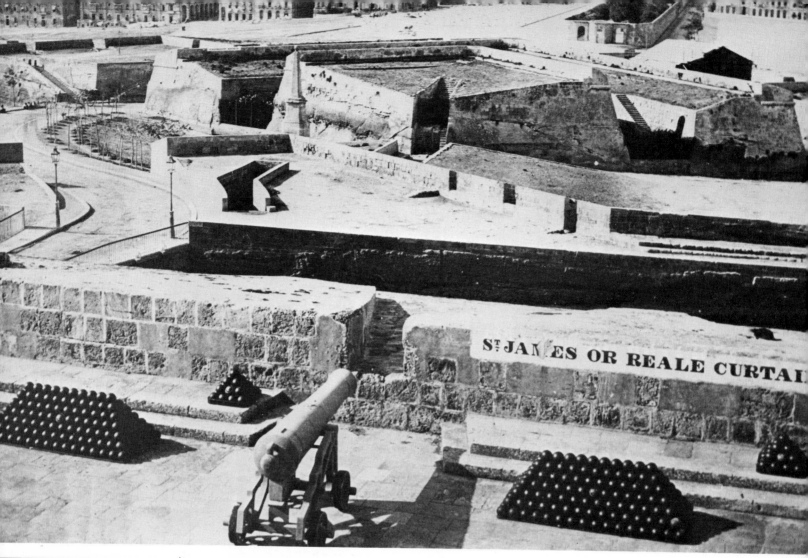

St JAMES OR REALE CURTAI

Fronte della Valletta con le strade coperte, trauerse et caponiere
47

The landfront at Valletta; (above) an old
photograph taken from the central curtain
showing the ravelin and, to the left, one of
the counterguards

A Ob. Castels Port
B Vnd. Castels Port
C Heydelberger Port
D Rhein Port
E Necker Port
F Necker Bruck

Die andere halbe der
Statt und Castels send
noch nicht gebaut
Die schwartz schattierte
aber send gebaute
gassen und ander abge-
brandt vnd die Weiß
Platz zeigen die Heuser
vnd gebaue so im brand
stehen blieben

across the Rhine was protected by a hornwork, a smaller one across the Neckar by a fleche. The landfront was stiffened on the right by a detached star-shaped fort standing in front of a large hornwork, and on the left by an impressive crown-work. The point of the peninsula had a small pentagonal fort. The main enceinte consisted of Italian bastions, two of which had their flanks protected by orillions. Beyond lay a continuous ditch with its counterscarp crowned by a covered way in which spaces, called places-of-arms, were left in the re-entrant angles for the assembly of troops. The exposed curtain walls of the citadel were protected by ravelins and, in two places, outworks in the form of lunettes extended the fortifications in depth.

Any wary city was proof against a *coup de main*. The major threat to its destruction lay in an organised siege when the attackers circumvallated the besieged place and proceeded either to starve it or to assault it in a systematic way. The credit for the evolution of a predetermined scientific method of approaching the walls of a fortified city must go to Vauban and his system will be described later. The main criteria were to cut trenches more or less parallel to the front of fortifications being attacked, so that besiegers could not be seen and thus flanked by artillery on the walls and bastions. These trenches were slowly pushed forward by short sections until the attackers were poised to assault a ravelin or a bastion which had to be breached before the defences of the town could be carried.

There are numerous descriptions of sieges in the seventeenth and eighteenth centuries, but none was more richly described nor more fiercely prosecuted than the great Turk-

Left
The defences of Mannheim; after Merian

*Philipville near Namur in Belgium; after
Braun and Hogenberg*

Right
*Breaching a bastion before attacking a
retrenchment; after Pietro Paolo Floriani*

ish siege of Vienna in 1683. The city was girdled by an irregular polygon consisting for the most part of obtuse-angled Italian bastions supported by ravelins in the ditch, part of which was flooded. To the north lay the Danube, at this point a maze of waterways and marshy islands, its waters touching the perimeter of the city. To the east was a semi-defended front with a wet ditch and beyond that a small tributary, the river Wien.

The defences were in the hands of a German military engineer called Rimpler. Having served with the Venetians at Candia in 1669 he was conversant with the Italian system. Four years later however he proposed his own system for a 'fortification with middle bastions'. No drawings were left, but in 1718 Leonhard Christoph Sturm published a drawing based on Rimpler's description. The system abolished curtain walls and substituted a tenaille trace, to the salient points of which were added acute-angled bastions, their faces forming an extension of supporting fausse-brayes. It was an elaborate system of defence in depth with double covered ways and several lines of ditches. Its main importance lies in the fact that its principles were adopted by Montalembert in the later eighteenth century, passing from him to become common practice among German military engineers of the mid-nineteenth century. Thus in the seventeenth century re-emerged a system which eventually superseded and made obsolete the Italian bastion trace. Rimpler appears to have had no opportunity to put his theory into practice, for the Vienna trace was straightforward and in line with current Italian thinking.

The Turks with a large force and some 250 cannon attacked through the suburbs from the south-west. In the drawings which remain their trenches appear like the maze of passages revealed in a sectioned anthill. By 17 July the city was invested and soon food ran short. The garrison, reduced from 11,000 to 4,000, was in a state of extreme exhaustion. Shingles were torn from the city roofs and burnt as flares on the battlements to illuminate any Turkish activity in the ditches. The usual stories of atrocities were circulated and the Turks were accused of seizing children from their mothers' arms and roasting them before fixing them on spear points to wave aloft as an earnest of the city's fate. The line of Turkish entrenchments had begun five miles from the walls of the fortress and it slowly closed in on the Burg and Löwel Bastions (marked A and B) and their intervening ravelin (marked D). There was mining and countermining and on 1 September one complete face of the ravelin erupted in smoke and flame. Pulverised continuously for 22 days and assaulted on at least 12 occasions, the ravelin finally fell. Then the Burg Bastion was breached and Turkish janissaries gained a foothold. The city seemed fated when at the eleventh hour the Duke of Lorraine and John Sobieski threw a relieving force across the Danube, using prefabricated bridges which had been constructed 15 miles upstream, and fell upon the Turkish army. In terror the Turks broke off their siege and fled, their commanding general being stripped of his insignia and ritually strangled. The threat of Turkish penetration in the west was countered in what an eminent Turkish historian has called 'the most important campaign in their history'.

If the main cities and towns of Europe were well-guarded by elaborate systems of fortification there were many less for-

The Turkish assault on Vienna; after Fer

tunate small towns open to attack. Those near the coasts of the Mediterranean were specially vulnerable as, particularly on dark nights, ships could approach silently, to descend undetected upon an isolated stretch of shore. An early warning system was needed to signal the approach of Turkish or corsair raiders in sufficient time to allow villagers to gather in the comparative safety provided by the communal defence of a tightly packed collection of houses, and to permit cavalry forces to hurry into position to repulse the advance or, often more effective, to impede withdrawal to the coast.

In the second half of the sixteenth century the long coastline of southern Italy began to be systematically planted with a line of coastal towers, fairly regularly spaced and supported at intervals by stronger forts. By 1569 some 13 towers covered 120 kilometres of the Apulian coast supported by ten forts, all in or near towns, centred on the fort at Bari. The forts and towers were sited so that messages could be rapidly transmitted to headquarters. Other towers, spaced about eight kilometres apart, covered the Gulf of Taranto and still more stretched up the Calabrian coast, along the seaboard of the Tyrrhenian Sea as far north as Rome.

Usually the towers were square, though round ones are sometimes found, and they were constructed of thick bat-

tered walls with few or no windows to illuminate the ground floor rooms. The main chamber was at first floor level, approached by ladder or drawbridge from a high stone staircase. The roof, strongly constructed to support cannon, was capped by machicolation, corbelled from the main walls and providing some defence for the base of the tower. The soldiers' accommodation was sufficiently isolated from attack so that in normal conditions an enemy would by-pass a tower rather than waste time on its bombardment: the essence of their raids being speed and surprise. It should also be remembered that ships of the period were not designed to fire broadsides. Usually frail galleys susceptible to fire from the shore, they invariably gave any coastal defences a wide berth.

In Malta an elaborate warning system was constructed by the Knights of St John. Towers were built there in medieval times but the systematic plan for the distribution of intercommunicating watchtowers did not originate until after the Great Siege of 1565. During the first half of the seventeenth century the Knights of St John constructed towers at all likely landing points. These towers were remarkably uniform in design, consisting of two rooms one above the other and space on the roof for two cannons which, during the day,

Left
*Charles V's bastions on the Fort at
Barletta, 1527*

Above
Fort at Barletta; aerial section

Above right
Castello at Bari

Right
*A watchtower on the coast at Gallipoli in
the heel of Italy*

Left
*The Wignacourt Tower at St Paul's Bay
in Malta*

A Maltese coastal watchtower

were used for signalling the approach of corsairs as well as to deter their landing. At night signal bonfires could be lit on the roof. Each tower was square and had a strongly scarped base culminating in a bold string course and a parapet with embrasures. The towers were designed for a garrison of four.

The most vulnerable areas were defended by forts, the earliest being the Wignacourt Tower built on St Paul's Bay in 1610. Fort St Lucian soon followed, with Fort St Thomas in 1614 and the fort on the island of Comino two years later. These buildings are strange. On first sight they give the impression of being square forts built on a full-bastioned trace, such as would have been expected after the visit to the island of such eminent Italian military engineers as Lanci, Serbelloni and Laparelli. However on close inspection it can be seen that the forts are square blocks with immensely thick battered walls. The corners of each fort were stiffened by towers whose walls rose vertically so that, although their bases touched the face of the curtains, their tops projected considerably in front of them, giving the impression of being bastions. This is particularly so in cases like Fort St Lucian where the towers in plan resemble true bastions, their faces being aligned with their neighbours' flanks. This is a device which Antonio da Sangallo carried out at the Fort at Nettuno 100 years earlier when he was attempting to evolve the true bastioned trace. It is incredible that the knights' knowledge of the theory of fortification should have been so rudimentary as to allow them to sanction these designs by local military engineers. There were no embrasures except at the tops of the towers and enfilade fire was an impossibility.

The forts at St Lucian and St Thomas were low-lying, near to the sea, and could thus not signal directly to the headquarters at Valletta. An intermediate signalling station had therefore to be selected and constructed. In 1614 the knights added two transepts and a dome to the fifteenth century church of St Gregory near Zejtun and incorporated high up within the thickness of the transept walls a narrow passage with two small windows sited directly on to the towers of these forts. From earliest times churches have been used as places of refuge and as stores for military equipment and ammunition, but it is interesting to find an example of a church being extended specifically for the purpose of fitting into an overall defence plan.

During the first half of the seventeenth century the Italians continued to dominate the scene and only gradually towards mid-century was their pre-eminent position taken over by the French. As a result of this Italian engineers began to turn to France for their ideas and the work of the French school, fully established by Vauban, held the stage almost unchallenged until the middle of the eighteenth century.

In the seventeenth century Malta remained a fruitful place of employment for the Italians. As the range and effectiveness of artillery improved, the depth of defences had to be increased to prevent the bombardment of the vital parts of a city, like the arsenal, the dockyard or the head-

quarters; and to blunt any assault so that a point of exhaustion might be reached before the final lines of defence were broken through. The Knights of Malta now found that they needed a second enceinte well beyond Laparelli's landfront of Valletta and a series of encircling bastions outside the sixteenth century defences of the harbours and the towns which bordered them. They first commissioned Pietro Paolo Floriani, a notable Italian engineer who had seen many battles and planned many fortresses and was the author of one of the most influential treatises of the period, *Difesa et offesa delle piazze* (Macerata 1630). Floriani submitted his first project in October 1635 and against considerable opposition his proposals were accepted and the Floriana lines were built. They consisted of a triple centre bastion supported by demi-bastions and a fortified wall which ran back along both coasts of the promontory to join the main defences of Valletta. The work of aggrandisement went on. Vincenzo Masculano da Firenzuola began a ring of fortifications on the hills of Santa Margherita and the Mandra in 1638 to strengthen the landward approach to the Three Cities which lie across the Grand Harbour from Valletta. Antonio Maurizio Valperga arrived in 1670, constructed a faussebraye and a new ditch in front of Floriani's bastions and ravelins and pushed out a noble hornwork, protected by a

Left
An early seventeenth century cannon of the Knights of St John

Above
St Lucian in Malta

Above right
Fort St Thomas in Malta

crownwork and a lunette, to act as a powerful outwork along the south-western edge of the lines. His client, the Grand Master Nicolas Cotoner, possessed of grandiose ideas, was not content with this, so Valperga then planned one of the most ambitious schemes in Europe. The Cottonera Lines, begun in 1670, stretch in a great arc to girdle the towns on the south-eastern seaboard of the Grand Harbour. At great expense eight bastions were built, but most of the vital outworks had to be omitted as the work drained the coffers of the knights and overstretched the ability of their troops to man and defend the lines. Finally built in durable stone, the gateways embellished with rich architectural trappings, the seventeenth century defences of Malta stand almost intact. Not overgrown by vegetation, nor concealed by suburban sprawl, they present to this day the finest examples of their type in Europe.

By the mid-seventeenth century the balance in the capabilities of attack and defence reached a climax. No other age saw the erection of such elaborate fortifications on so vast a scale, and on no earlier occasion were they so surely doomed. Much of the credit for both situations must go to Vauban. This is why he is important.

Left
The Floriana lines in Malta showing the
hornwork and crownwork on the left : the
lines shown projecting beyond the glacis
are countermines

Below left
The Cottonera Lines in Malta

Romano Carrapecchia's Zabbar Gate in the
Cottonera Lines, 1675

Left
An ornate gatework by Wilhelm Dilich,
1640

Below left
Section through a drawbridge and fortified
gateway by Dilich

Portrait of Vauban

Sébastien le Prestre de Vauban was born in Burgundy on 15 May 1633. Before his eighteenth birthday he had joined the army to rise, in 1703, to the rank of Marshal of France. During his long life as a military engineer he worked on more than 160 fortresses and directed 40 sieges, all of which were successful. In the first five years of his army service he was wounded on five occasions. At the age of 70, after returning from his last siege, he wrote *Traité de l'attaque des places*. It was a secret document not intended for publication, but produced for the use of the Duke of Burgundy, grandson of Louis XIV. In the preface Vauban wrote 'May it please you to keep it to yourself, and let no one else have it . . .'. Nearly three years later, and shortly before he died, he wrote *Traité de la défence des places*. In his behaviour and his writings there constantly appeared his maxim 'never do uncovered and by force what can be done by industry'.

Vauban's name is usually associated with three systems of defence. In fact he did not lay these down; they were deduced by his pupils and followers from the fortresses that Vauban had designed, for he had written 'the art of fortifying does not consist in rules and systems, but solely in good sense and experience'.

Vauban's first system, which he used in more than 30 places he fortified, does not vary greatly from the traditional pattern then evolving in the hands of French and Italian military engineers. It consisted of a front of about 330 metres with generous bastions and large flanks making obtuse angles with both faces of the bastions and the curtain walls. The curtains were protected by low tenailles joined by a caponier to a ravelin lying farther out in the ditch. Beyond lay the covered way, interspersed by traverses to pro-

Right
*Model of a new town of Neuf-Brisach
(Neuf-Brisach Museum)*

Below
Vauban's First Method (left) *and
Vauban's Third Method; after John
Muller, 1746*

tect his troops, and places-of-arms in the salient and re-entrant angles. Vauban's caponier was merely a protected bombproof passage joining the tenaille to the ravelin. Only in the nineteenth century did caponiers and counterscarp galleries usurp the ditch-flanking functions of the bastions. Caponiers gradually assumed colossal proportions at places like Posen (1828) and Dover Castle, becoming many-tiered multi-gun keeps.

Vauban's second system was the result of his practical progress in siegecraft which induced him to modify the trace of his fortresses. Discovering that whenever a bastion was captured the loss of the town followed, he transformed his bastions into counterguards separated by a ditch from the curtain wall which was strengthened at the corners by two-storey polygonal towers, stoutly constructed to contain cannon enclosed within bombproof casemates and firing through embrasures. Vauban's third system was his most complex and was only used once, at Neuf-Brisach. It consisted of a front of considerable depth, with cavaliers on the bastions, counterguards and tenailles, a ravelin with its own counter-guard and large re-entrant places-of-arms. It was expensive and was not employed after Vauban's time, but fortunately there remains an almost complete example of this work preserved at Neuf-Brisach. Under the terms of the Treaty of Ryswick France lost Brisach and the ground on the right bank of the Rhine. Louis XIV, realising that his flank was exposed, commissioned Vauban to design a new fortress within French territory. In 1698 Vauban submitted three projects, of which one was chosen, and the place was put in a state of defence by 1706. It was originally designed to contain only military personnel, but the octagonal space within

the bastions was converted into a gridiron town with a large central square.

This scant description does not do justice to the elaborate scientific nature of Vauban's constructions, but as his fame rested upon them, practically every military engineer of note who followed described his systems in considerable detail. They became the imperative solution for the French school of engineers.

Vauban's fame rests unjustly on his military architecture, for it was he who swung the balance in favour of the attack, establishing its superiority over defence for nearly 200 years.

Before Vauban's time the attack on fortresses had been unsystematic. The lack of method was evident in the Turkish assault on Vienna in 1683. In a memorandum written in 1704 he decried the haphazard and unsystematic character of attack. 'When we succeed,' he wrote, 'it is rather owing to the weakness of the enemy than to our own merit.' He probably remembered the sight of English grenadiers marching across a half mile of open ground with drums beating and colours flying. 'I never saw anything like it, or even approaching it; for the magnitude of the blunder, I mean, not for the grandeur of the action, for I find that too senseless to admire it.' His system of attack was based on the use of parallels which he first used effectively at the siege of Maestricht (1673). Starting about 600 metres out from the fortress to be attacked, and working at night, he detailed small detachments of men, 25 and an officer, to open up trenches running parallel to the front he wished to attack. On the second night he constructed batteries whose guns were intended to keep the defenders quiet. Then began zigzag approaches, each approach concealed from the besieged; by

Right
The fortifications of Lille, showing the citadel on the right, two hornworks on the upper left of the picture and an assault on a ravelin and two tenaillons at the bottom of the picture

Below
The Colmar Gate at Neuf-Brisach

Far right
Vauban's curtain and bastion on the Colmar front

the fourth night the approaches had reached halfway, when a second parallel trench was constructed. More zigzags followed and by the ninth or tenth night the third parallel was cut at the foot of the glacis. The artillery next opened up a breach in the ravelin and then in the bastion. The crowning of the covered way was the most dangerous task (at Philipsburgh in 1676 it had cost the lives of 1,200 men) and the work was best done systematically. The attackers then descended into the ditch, taking cover behind the rubbish which had been brought down in the breach of the ravelin and the bastion. In ordinary circumstances the assault on the fortress would commence at dawn on the twentieth day of the investment.

Not many sieges can have progressed with this clockwork precision, but the vindication of Vauban's system of attack is surely the complete success of all the sieges which he himself directed.

Colonel John Jones, of the Corps of Engineers, summed up Vauban's contribution. 'By the middle of the sixteenth and the commencement of the seventeenth century, works were so well covered and so skilfully disposed, that the defence of towns obtained a momentary superiority over the rude efforts of the attack as then practised – for example the Dutch against Philip II and III. Unhappily, however, for this pre-eminence, Louis XIV appeared personally on the scene, and brought to the attack of fortresses a preparation in ordnance, ammunition and materials, so vast and costly, as even at this day to excite astonishment; and thus supported, the genius of one man, Vauban, perfected in the first offensive campaign of that Monarch, a covered mode of attack, by a combination of Labour and Science, which rendered easy, by the steady advance of a few well-trained brave men, the reduction of places capable of defying for ever the open violence of multitudes. These increased means of attack caused the art of concealment to be further studied, till at length, in well constructed fortresses, not a single wall remained exposed to view, and the sap and the mine became as indispensably necessary as the gun and the mortar to the success of a besieger.'

Vauban's methods were perpetuated, with minor modifications, by numerous French engineers, the most noteworthy being Louis de Cormontaingne whose assault went in on the twenty-second day of the siege. Cormontaingne's *Architecture Militaire* was published as a secret document in 1714, but the information was soon stolen and an unauthorised edition came out abroad in 1741, followed by

The inner gate at Longwy by Vauban

Attack on the ravelin of a fortress showing the position of the besieger's batteries and his parallels and saps

others. Although he was not a very original thinker two of his ideas merit attention. He revived a notion popularised by the Italians that a straight line of defence is most easily held, because broad obtuse-angled bastions could be covered by ravelins and could thus not be enfiladed by enemy fire. He therefore recommended a large triangular fortress with a strong citadel placed at one salient angle, arguing that the enemy would then be forced to attack one of the remaining two angle bastions. Defence could be concentrated here and the bastions covered by a narrow projecting hornwork. Cormontaingne also worked out his 'scale of comparison'. This was a device whereby the strength of a fortress, and thus the number of days it could be expected to hold out, was calculated against a hypothetical attack, assuming that the besieger followed the general rules of the game. The disadvantage of this scale was that once the strength of a fortress was known few commanders would feel in honour bound to resist an attack beyond the time predicted for its success.

The work of these men is splendidly preserved in a series of large scale models which are still housed in Les Invalides in Paris. These depict the most important fortified cities built along the Franco-Belgian frontiers from the seventeenth to the nineteenth centuries, and one shows in great detail the devastation wrought on the citadel at Antwerp in the protracted siege of 1830–32.

The Dutch were fortunate in living in an area of low-lying ground most of which could be easily flooded by the rivers that traversed it or by the sea. This gave the inhabitants an advantage which they quickly seized in the wars of independence when meagre garrisons held at bay the full highly organised force of the Spanish imperial army. The Dutch school of military engineering began to rise to a position of importance in the middle years of the sixteenth century. Adam Freitag published his *New and Enlarged Military Architecture* in Leyden in 1631. The defences of Alkmaar date from 1573–75, Elburg from 1580, and Jacob Kemps fortified Heusden in 1581, the defences of which are now being painstakingly restored to their original state.

Naarden is an old Dutch town, walled from the middle ages, several times captured and its defences rebuilt. In 1673 William III ordered a reconstruction with fortifications based on the New Dutch System. The architect was Adrian Dortsman and the military engineer Willem Paen. Naarden's defences were again brought up to date during the Franco-Prussian War when mortar casemates were constructed. Be-

cause of its strategic position, the fortifications were kept in operation until quite recently and this accounts for their remarkable state of preservation. The seventeenth century bastioned trace and the water defences also remain intact and the town is a magnificent example of its period.

Centuries of war threw up many able Dutch military engineers, but the most important was undoubtedly Mennon, Baron van Coehorn. His strength was often pitted against Vauban for whom he was a worthy rival. The two men held almost diametrically opposed attitudes to attack and defence. Where Vauban was cautious, slow and thorough, Coehorn sacrificed everything to surprise, speed and a murderous artillery bombardment. His particular passion was for the deployment of numerous small mortars of a type which still carry his name.

Left
A ravelin and wet ditch at Heusden

The fortified town of Heusden in Holland

An early writer compared the two men. 'Vauban, employing no more guns than were necessary, using all his influence to restrain his troops, not allowing them to advance except under cover, and bringing them in this way to the foot of each work, had made it his study and pride to spare them; and had done this without slacking the siege. Coehorn, accumulating ordnance, sending the troops across the open to make assaults at a distance, and sacrificing everything to his eagerness to shorten the siege and to scare and frighten the defenders, had economised neither money nor men, nor in fact time.' The critic was in fact a Frenchman, but he underestimated Coehorn whose career was remarkably successful. One of his fortresses, Namur, was captured by Vauban who refortified it. Three years later Coehorn recaptured it. He was appointed a corps commander in the Duke of Marlborough's army and fortified numerous cities, some with complete success.

In 1685 he published his three systems of fortification for Dutch sites where water was readily available to flood the ditches and the surrounding countryside. In plan his first method looked remarkably like Vauban's but the similarity was superficial. Coehorn's bastions were more complex (marked A and B). In front (XG–XH) lay a dry ditch before the outer face of the bastion was reached. A bonnet (E–F) hung above the salient angle of the bastion and was joined to the inner bastion by a low bombproof caponier. The flanks of the bastions were large and deep with space and embrasures for adequate artillery defence, and the orillions became strong stone towers containing magazines. The orillions were constructed in the form of hollow counterforts consisting of several membranes so that, if the enemy's

Naarden in Holland: (above right) *the flank of a bastion;* (right) *the curved flank of a bastion according to the New Dutch System, and* (opposite above) *aerial view*

Opposite left
Coehorn's First Method; after John Muller

Opposite right
The type of bastion adopted by Coehorn as illustrated in Dilich's Peribologia, *1640*

Cochorn's First Method.

Plate XII.

Fig. 2.

guns broke through one skin of masonry, he was faced with the necessity of destroying the next, and so on. Deep counterforts, not filled with earth, had a great advantage. If they collapsed under bombardment the minimum of rubble slid down into the ditch providing scant cover for the besieger's assault troops. All Coehorn's systems had elaborate outworks to expose the enemy everywhere to cross fire, and these works were succoured by means of boats. Wet ditches were always a problem for although they deterred an attack, except in the depth of winter, they made it very difficult for the defenders to withdraw from an untenable position. A last-ditch stand in the outworks was not normally required in the defence of a fortress whose defences were designed to absorb the blows of the attack by means of a succession of defensive rings. Defending troops had to retire from the outworks in any boats that were available and undamaged, carrying with them their wounded; alternatively they were forced to swim for their lives.

Coehorn's second and third systems, although carefully worked out, were never applied, for the defensive rings required such a vast amount of land that the area remaining within the fortification would have been almost too small to accommodate and arm a garrison sufficient for their defence. Coehorn in 1688 fortified Bergen-op-Zoom and made it one of the strongest Dutch fortresses, secured on the west by the estuary of the Scheldt and on the east by the lines of Steenbergen. The defences proved their worth 125 years later when, occupied by a small French garrison of about 2,500 men, the town was surprised in a night assault by British troops under the command of Sir Thomas Graham. The British corps consisted of about 10,000 men. Aided by winter

conditions, for the dykes refused to function adequately and flood the surrounding ground, parties of the British broke into the place, but the defenders, thinly supporting the outworks (Fort d'Eau had only 60 men in it), used the fortifications as a natural deterrent and concentrated their small force to counter-attack any threatened position. By these means the attackers were cut off, killed or captured.

Throughout the eighteenth century the French school of military engineers was held in great repute and was employed in numerous commissions beyond the frontier. Two names stand out. Montalembert, their most controversial figure, and Carnot.

Marc René, Marquis de Montalembert, was born in 1714. When eighteen years old he joined the army and was present at many of the sieges of the Seven Years' War. Brought up in an age when Vauban had perfected the art of attack, Montalembert turned his attention to the needs of the defence in an attempt to redress the balance. Whereas most of the French engineers were prepared to stick with absurd obstinacy to the traditions of fortification evolved by Vauban and his contemporaries, Montalembert searched desperately for other means of defence. Understandably his ideas faced opposition from his fellow engineers and his progress on the ladder of promotion was prejudiced by his forthright opinions. Like many innovators his life could have passed unnoticed and his recommendations consigned to oblivion were it not for the fact that his suggestions were accepted with alacrity by the rising power of Prussia and transmitted to the German states during a period of feverish rearmament in the nineteenth century. In 1761 Montalembert was appointed

Plan of Bergen-op-Zoom, showing the Fort d'Eau on the left; after John T. Jones

Coehorn's Third System; after John Muller

governor of the Ile of Oléron and put out to graze. The last 38 years of his life were spent writing the 11 thick volumes of his *Fortification Perpendiculaire*. He objected strongly to the bastion trace, pointing out that curtain walls were quite useless. These had always been recognised as the weak points, the most negative element in the defence, requiring all the other works to cover them. The ability of guns on the bastions to pour enfilade fire across the front from their faces and flanks had been an advantage when the range of cannon was short. When a greater concentration of more accurate weapons became available, cross fire did not make full use of the effective range of which the weapons were capable. Montalembert therefore substituted a tenaille trace. The idea had been advocated years earlier. Both Italian and German engineers had suggested its use in the sixteenth century but it had never really become popular. However its revival seems to have been due to Heinrich von Landsberg (1670–1746) who in 1712 was probably the first engineer to point out the defensive qualities of the tenaille trace in *Nouveaux plans et projets de fortification, pour défendre et attaquer les places*.

The tenaille trace consisted of a series of triangular redans, abutting each other at right angles to form a continuous saw-edged front. Beyond the tenaille trace lay two lines of counterguards and behind it stood strong, two-storey circular towers, each containing 24 guns capable of firing out across the countryside. The system therefore had four distinct enceintes which, for their subjugation required four successive breaches. It was introduced in 1776 and is normally referred to as 'perpendicular fortification'. In the following year Montalembert produced his 'polygonal fortification'

Montalembert's multi-gun tower and caponier; after Lendy

Opposite
Polygonal fortification according to Montalembert

which contained immensely strong caponiers, three storeys high, armed with 27 guns in casemates and numerous infantry loopholes. The caponier, intended up to the time of Vauban as a secure means of communication between two defensive works, thus became a strongpoint in its own right.

It was these two last features, the multi-gun tower and the multi-gun caponier, which were taken up and developed with such enthusiasm by the Germans and the Austrians. The gun, protected by a bombproof casemate, its embrasures covered by solid shutters and designed for the minimum usable aperture, was the foundation of Montalembert's defensive system. Casemates were not new; they had been advocated by Dürer and other early engineers but they had fallen out of favour with the development of the bastion. However with the development of ricochet fire, said to have

been first used effectively by Vauban at Philipsburgh in 1688, the need was felt for more adequate protection of guns and crews. Fortunately the new gun carriages required a much smaller complement of men. However because their size was reduced, guns could be placed closer together to increase the concentration of fire and so became an even more attractive target for retaliation.

Carnot sensed the frustration felt by the aged general whose recommendations had not found favour in France. In a letter he advised Montalembert to 'look to posterity to render you the justice that is due to you'.

Lazare-Nicolas Carnot rose to importance as a result of the French Revolution. From being a captain of engineers he became a colleague of Robespierre and in 1800 Secretary of War to Napoleon Bonaparte, at whose request he wrote *De la défense des places fortes* in 1810. Carnot excelled as an organiser, but possessed sufficient foresight to accept innovation. In 1783 he had been working on captive balloons which, ten years later, were first used as a means of reconnaissance. He attacked the conservative attitude of the French Corps of Engineers and, drawing heavily on Montalembert, advocated the construction of a string of tough fortresses to guard the frontier.

Carnot's eminence was shortlived. Napoleon disregarded his advice (not to risk his all in one battle) and after Waterloo Carnot was forced to flee from France. He raised three main points in his treatise, each subsequently open to criticism. He advocated vertical fire from mortars in retrenched casemates, hidden from the enemy and yet capable of lobbing their shells over the work which protected them. Secondly he realised that with the introduction of ricochet fire the covered way had largely lost its value and would not protect his troops. He therefore recommended countersloping glacis, clear ground which sloped up from the ditch towards the open country. An attacking enemy would be caught in full view on this open gentle inclination. Thirdly he recommended the use of detached walls, a device adopted by the Austrians at Verona where the scarp walls were not tied back

Opposite
Fort St Louis at Toulon and (below)
Fort Manoel in Malta

Below left
*Battery at Comino near Malta ; aerial
section*

Fort Tigné ; from an old photograph

to the earthen rampart, but stood free. The walls were pierced by several tiers of loopholes through which infantry could fire muskets or grenades at the attackers exposed on the countersloping glacis.

In practice the French engineers clung to their traditional concepts, but their reputation was still high and they were invited by the Knights of Malta to carry out most of their eighteenth century projects of fortification. Fort Manoel is a typical example of their work. It was designed by the French engineers de Tigné and Gion de Mondion who arrived on the island early in 1715. The fort was square with four corner bastions, the cheapest solution for providing anything like a reasonable space for an adequate garrison within the walls of the enceinte. The curtain of the landfront was protected by a tenaille and a ravelin in the dry ditch, the adjacent curtains by lunettes connected by caponiers, and there were the usual Vauban devices such as traverses, a wide covered way and adequate places-of-arms on the landward front. Fort Manoel is a fine example of a pattern of no great originality repeated elsewhere on innumerable occasions.

In the middle years of the eighteenth century the Knights began to stiffen their defences along the coasts of Malta by building, at vulnerable points, infantry lines and a number of semi-circular batteries of a type evolved by the French at the end of the previous century. Fort St Louis (1692–97) at Toulon is a typical prototype.

The Maltese batteries all followed this pattern. Built on the seashore, they had a semi-circular front of between four and eight gun positions firing through embrasures in the parapet, and the garrison was accommodated in two rooms at the back of the fort, the walls lined with loopholes for muskets. The middle of the landfront was protected by a redan similarly loopholed.

The last important fort built by the Knights before they were thrown off the island by Napoleon's troops was Fort Tigné. Begun in 1792, this coast defence fort was designed by A. S. de Tousard. It was an unusual work which later received considerable praise from both French and British engineers. It consisted of a quadrangular enceinte with embrasures for cannon, a wide ditch with loopholed galleries in the angles of the ditch to provide for its defence, and a maze of countermines laid beyond these galleries to be exploded in the event of an assault. In one corner of the quadrangle stood an isolated tower, two storeys high and 18 metres in diameter, approached by a draw-bridge and intended as a defensible keep, a last defence in the event of a siege.

The square Castillo de San Marcos in Florida

Far left
Fort Raleigh; plan

Left
Fort at Puerto Rico; plan

The maritime nations of the west penetrated along the coasts of Africa and Asia and into the hinterland of South America, establishing commercial bases which had in time to be defended against the greed of others. So European ideas on fortification spread across the world and little forts sprang up on distant shores, simplified models of those in use at home. The Portuguese were among the earliest to build colonial forts. By the end of the fifteenth century they were beginning to fortify the West African coast. A century later they built Fort Jesus at Mombasa designed by Joao Batista Cairato. It was a square fort with bastions, some of whose flanks were covered by orillions. It was a sort of caricature of Italian practice, had strange cavaliers raised in the salient angles of two bastions and an entrance gate formed in the flank of a third. Macao on the China coast was strongly fortified after the unsuccessful Dutch attack in 1622. The Monte Fort, a typical square work with four corner bastions, was a simplified version of Fort Manoel built a century later. An almost identical fort, the Castillo de San Marcos, was erected by the Spaniards on the coast of Florida in 1672, and is now splendidly preserved by the United States National Park Service.

The British also built their forts, at first small and somewhat primitive like Fort Raleigh (1585) on Roanoke Island in the new land called Virginia. Its plan is strange, perhaps illustrating the primitive knowledge of fortification held by English sailors and early colonists. It consisted of a diamond overlying a square, with one corner of the diamond converted into a rudimentary heart-shaped bastion of a type that Rogers had used at Boulogne and another point cut short to form the entrance to the fort. Stranger still is Ralph Lane's fort at Puerto Rico built in the same year. There are similarities, for this fort also consisted of a diamond overlying a square, but at Puerto Rico one salient angle was converted into a spur, a device used consistently by English colonial fort builders on the west coast of Africa, and the opposite salient was omitted, to be replaced by two re-entrant arches in the middle of which lay the entrance.

By the eighteenth century British engineers, if not recommending valid innovations, were at least building in an accepted European manner. Fort Anomabu on the Gold Coast, begun in 1756, consisted of a square plan with corner bastions following a well-established tradition.

Elsewhere the French were busy consolidating their settlements. On the rivers which run between New York and Montreal they built, in 1755, Fort Ticonderoga, a square-bastioned structure with triangular works called demi-lunes placed in front of the north and west curtain, a ditch, a rudimentary covered way and the semblance of a glacis. The fort was originally constructed of logs backed by earthen ramparts but was later reconstructed in stone. At Louisburg, commanding the Cabot Strait, the French built their main stronghold on the North American continent, a port with its landfront protected by a fully bastioned front. Montreal was also defended and Quebec had four large bastions and two demi-bastions running across the Heights of Abraham. Within this enceinte lay a second line of partly constructed defences, with broad obtuse-angled bastions and, at the core of the city dominating the Heights, stood the star-shaped fort of St Louis which was later converted into a British strongpoint. No wonder Major-General Wolfe hesitated to commit his troops to a frontal attack on so strong a

Below
Fort Ticonderoga; bird's eye view

Right
The citadel at Quebec; plan

Opposite top
Fort William at Calcutta

Opposite below
Fort St George at Madras

fortification, and instead chose to mount one of the most brilliant amphibious operations in history, scaling the precipitous cliffs and attacking at a point the French considered to be inaccessible, to earn that famous tribute from the king: 'Mad is he?' asked George II, 'I wish to heaven he would bite some of my other generals!' In 1818 Lt-Col E. W. Durnford submitted his plan for enlarging Fort St Louis and converting it into the citadel of Quebec making it in its day the most formidable fortress in North America. New bastions were built, strengthened on two sides by counterguards, and three ravelins were constructed in front of the curtain walls.

In India the British strengthened their defences in the eighteenth century. Clive's two preoccupations after recapturing Calcutta in 1757 were to provide an army strong enough to defend the East India Company's possessions and to build a fortress sufficiently capacious to hold that army. The old fort was quite inadequate, so John Brohier was instructed to prepare plans for the new Fort William on a virgin site by the river. The designs were executed in two

months, and the trace followed in its broad outlines the work of Cormontaingne and the French school of engineers. Brohier struggled with the problem of inadequate labour handling unfamiliar materials in a building enterprise that was without precedent. He became involved in the corruption which was a part of Indian life and was arrested for fraud in 1760. A succession of engineers struggled in an attempt to redress the situation. Work dragged on till 1774 and it took a further seven years to fully arm the fort, which became the first substantial fortress in British India.

At Madras on the Coromandel coast Patrick Ross began a complete reconstruction of Fort St George in 1770, laying out a trace in the form of a large semi-octagon, its back facing the sea.

The British were slowly forging an engineer corps capable of holding its own with its European counterparts, but several generations were to pass before it could assume some position of eminence, and then mainly in the field of coastal defence.

1 *De Gomme's plan for Liverpool*   2 *Fort Tilbury on the Thames (Crown Copyright)*   3 *The citadel at Ayr in Scotland*   4 *Fort Cumberland at Portsmouth; plan*   5 *Fort Augustus at Inverness; plan*   6 *An embrasure covering the ditch at Fort Cumberland*

5

6

The Civil War of 1642 found Britain with less than a handful of towns protected by permanent fortifications. The realisation of this deficiency threw the country into a frenzy as citadels and earthworks were hastily constructed to resist attack. For Liverpool Sir Bernard de Gomme produced a plan in 1644 for enclosing the medieval castle within a quadrangular-bastioned trace from which would extend a curtain wall punctuated by seven bastions in an arc to be terminated on the banks of the river Mersey by two demi-bastions. In 1652, with the declaration of a commonwealth between England and Scotland, construction began on four Scottish citadels, Ayr, Inverness, Leith and St Jonston. They were designed in a grandiose style by British standards to impose a protectorate upon a largely hostile population. At Ayr the citadel formed an elongated hexagon with earthen ramparts, a wet ditch which could be drained by a cunette, a covered way with small places-of-arms in the shallow re-entrant angles and a glacis. The work was designed by Hans Ewald Tessin.

De Gomme was a Dutch engineer who had served with the royalists in the Civil War. Understandably his opportunity came with the restoration of the monarchy when Charles II made him engineer-in-chief to undertake, in 1665, a major programme of refortification for Portsmouth. Working on the original enceinte he remodelled the bastions and added four large ravelins to a wider moat. As one might expect from a Dutch engineer water was to play a vital part in his defensive systems. The work of reconstruction took over 20 years to complete and rather ironically was largely carried out by Dutch prisoners of war. This design made Portsmouth the strongest fortress in Britain, a position of eminence it was

to retain with modifications up to the abandonment of permanent fortifications at the end of the Second World War. In 1673 de Gomme designed a regular pentagonal citadel at Dublin, its trace modelled on the New Dutch System. His best-preserved work is at Tilbury where in 1670 he constructed a regular pentagonal fort dependent upon broad water defences formed by a double ditch and surrounding marshy meadows. In Dutch style, sluices regulated the level of the water in the moat. The government had been badly frightened by the devastating Dutch naval raid up the Thames in 1667. The river's sole protection was the little round-fronted blockhouse constructed by Henry VIII and later incorporated as a cavalier into one of de Gomme's bastions. The new fort was designed to prevent any repetition of the affair. De Gomme's drawing shows a fausse-braye within the inner moat, a ravelin interrupting the system of drawbridges on the landward side and covering the main gate, and a broad covered way with places-of-arms at both the salient and re-entrant angles. As one would expect, the river frontage was most strongly armed with its parapets pierced by numerous embrasures.

Except for the Scottish troubles Britain in the eighteenth century felt fairly secure from foreign invasion and saw no cause to emulate her neighbours in the construction of vastly expensive fortifications around her cities and coastline. Her powerful fleet had by then become the first line of defence. With the exception of the stiffening of the Portsmouth defences by the construction of Fort Cumberland, a regular pentagonal work, in 1786, the sole outlet for British military engineers on home soil lay in the north of Scotland. Fort Augustus was built between 1729 and 1742, designed in the form of a square-bastioned fort by John Romer. In order to end once and for all the threat of jacobite uprisings the British government embarked upon a policy of fortress building in the highlands. Part of the work consisted of reconstructing forts that had been slighted in the uprising of 1745–46 and part in the erection of new works. The most imposing of the new structures was Fort George at the entrance to the Moray Firth which leads up to Inverness. This fort still remains in its entirety, splendidly preserved. Fort George was designed in 1747 by William Skinner on a narrow spur of land projecting into the sea so that, like Valletta some 200 years earlier, the main task for the engineer lay in providing a strong landfront across the neck of the peninsula with adequate direct fire out to sea from the point. The landfront consists of two full bastions lying behind a broad ditch. From their salient angles, batardeaux extend to the covered way to control the water level in the ditch. The entrance, marked by a monumental gate and approached by a timber bridge, is covered by a bold ravelin supported by two lunettes which stand in the re-entrant places-of-arms. Sallyports give access to places-of-arms situated on the foreshore and the long sides of the fort are punctuated by broad bastions and terminated by smaller demi-bastions. Around the ramparts runs a broad terreplein, linking the bastions and the curtain walls and approached from the parade ground by gentle ramps up which artillery pieces could be manhandled. The guns fired through embrasures in the parapets and the flanks of the bastions provided positions for enfilading the adjoining faces. At the angles of the bastions echaugettes, or round sentry boxes, are corbelled out to survey the surrounding terrain and from them a passage leads through the earthwork of the parapet to the terreplein. If the fort shows no great originality it is at least a competent design beautifully detailed and excellently constructed. William Skinner certainly knew his job. By 1769 Fort George was complete, the last major fortification to be constructed in Britain for nearly a century, if one excepts the work on the Western Heights at Dover, begun in 1803 in the face of a threatened French invasion, and designed to transform the hill into an entrenched camp for 5,000–6,000 men.

Fort George at Inverness

Chapter five

THE NINETEENTH CENTURY: ESCALATION

The early nineteenth century is an age of contradictions. It attempts to reconcile the flights of fantasy of the early gothic revival with the stark reality of industrial revolution, the heroics of Balaclava with the murderous slogging at Inkerman and Sebastopol, and the image of a chivalrous past with the hard practicality of survival under conditions of modern war. It was an age when beer barons, slate magnates and extravagant monarchs built fortified residences for the fun of the game. The mock-castle imparted or implied the semblance of an aristocratic background for an occupant all too often feeling a little uncertain in a newly created position of wealth or power. It has been shown how the Marquis of Bute reconstructed Castell Coch with painstaking authenticity in 1875, and how Napoleon III had commissioned Viollet-le-Duc to carry out what amounted to the rebuilding of Pierrefonds Castle in 1858. Most of the British clients seem to have gone for the Norman style which pushed their respectability back to the very beginning of the middle ages. One of the best examples is Penrhyn Castle, designed by Thomas Hopper in 1827 in a perfect romantic landscape, its great keep modelled on Rochester. The building cost Lord Penrhyn half a million pounds. These romantic castles were part of a new enthusiasm for the medieval world which found

expression in Walter Scott's novel *Ivanhoe*. The most extravagant demonstration in this world of make-believe was the fairy castle commissioned by Ludwig II of Bavaria. After seeing Louis Napoleon's work at Pierrefonds, Ludwig resolved to emulate him in an even more extravagant and fanciful manner. Neuschwanstein was begun in 1869 to the designs of Eduard Riedel, but subsequently developed by others. It has been aptly described as 'one of the most fascinating toys in the world'.

The opening of the new century found Europe in the grip of war and Britain involved for the first time for nearly 100 years in the preparation and deployment of an army on a continental scale. In the Peninsula Wellington's army withdrew to the prepared Lines of Torres Vedras, thrown up in 1810 to cover the roads to Lisbon. To their astonishment the French were checked and left exposed to starve on inhospitable slopes through a fierce winter, whilst the British army sat snugly recuperating behind the security of the lines. Their construction had been planned by Colonel Fletcher as one of the most ambitious secret projects of the war. The works, which are normally classed as field fortifications, were sited with great care to take full advantage of the

Penrhyn Castle

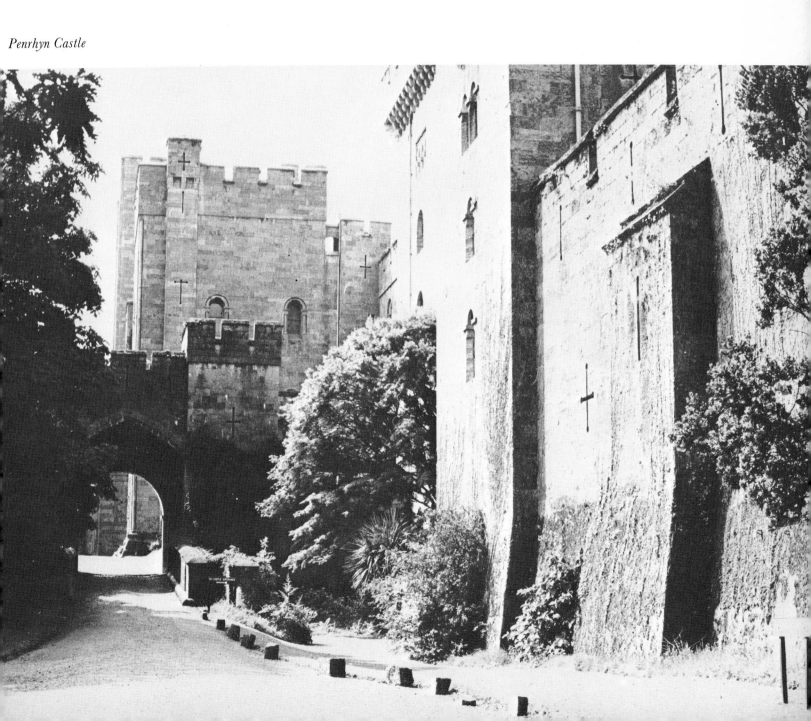

Redoubts on the lines of Torres Vedras;
after Jones

An early nineteenth century 32-pounder naval gun at Deal Castle

The attack on Burgos; after Jones

rocky front which stretched for a length of 25 kilometres from the Tagus to the Atlantic and guarded the passes through which the roads ran to the capital. The main front consisted of 59 redoubts mounting 232 guns and armed with a garrison of 17,500 men. In advance of this stood further redoubts forming valuable outposts. Lisbon lay 19 kilometres to the rear. Five months after commencement the works were handed over to Captain John T. Jones who later became one of the most important writers on English fortifications and whose descriptions of the sieges of the Napoleonic Wars are invaluable. Wellington fell back through heavy rain and swollen rivers, withdrawing his 22,000 infantry and 3,000 cavalry with a similar number of Portuguese to the security of the lines where he exploded the myth that any army which holds its ground must surely be beaten. From this position he turned withdrawal into victory so that Jones was able to write: 'It is not, perhaps, too much to add, that this failure before Lisbon gave a fatal blow to the general belief of French invincibility, and taught oppressed Europe to resist and become free'

The redoubts varied in size and shape according to their position of importance and the ground upon which each was sited. They show a remarkable adaptability on the part of the British engineers who were perhaps less inhibited by a conservative education than their French counterparts.

The defence of Lisbon demonstrated four points. It showed that in certain circumstances defence, after a century of reverses, could once more prove successful. It illustrated the usefulness of secrecy. It pointed to the value of the irregular disposition of fortifications to suit ground conditions. It also proved to be the forerunner of the idea of using

*Festung Ehrenbreitstein at Koblenz: rear
façade of the curtain*

Overleaf
*The rear of a caponier at Ehrenbreitstein
and plan*

isolated forts, supported by a field army, to bar an enemy's advance. Although these defences have been called the Lines of Torres Vedras, they were in reality embryonic barrier-forts, a system which was to find its fullest expression in the Maginot Line.

Throughout the Peninsular War the British were sadly short of sappers and miners, and those they had were expended at a prodigal rate. In the following years the British army was forced to besiege a number of Spanish towns garrisoned by the French behind regular fronts of fortification stiffened with formidable outworks. Credit for the success of many of the assaults must go to the expenditure of life which Wellington, fighting against time, was prepared to accept. Badajoz, Ciudad Rodrigo and Burgos were all besieged, the first on three occasions. According to Jones as many men were lost before Badajoz as would have been sufficient for ten sieges undertaken with science and careful labour. His experience in battle made his observations on the attack of fortresses highly pertinent.

Other British engineers were forging a workable knowledge of the science of fortification. C. W. Pasley's *Course of Elementary Fortification* is one of the first of a long line of reliable textbooks intended for the training of the professional engineer, books which towards the end of the century became the standard manuals of field and permanent fortification. Pasley opened with a short history of the Corps of Engineers and its predecessors and then, having defined terms, for the art and science of fortification was rapidly evolving its own specialised semantics within the English language, he went on to describe the geometrical methods involved in the setting out of fortresses, leaning heavily on the

practice of Vauban. His book is the first fully comprehensive English work. Lt Henry Yule (1820–89) of the Bengal Engineers, later to be knighted and best-known for his glossary of Anglo-Indian words, produced in 1851 his *Fortification for Officers of the Army and Students of Military History*. This is another thorough book on the subject and it includes an historical study of the development of fortification, probably the earliest example in English. Meanwhile in 1849 James Fergusson had published *An Essay on a Proposed New System of Fortifications*. He was an architect and somewhat diffident at expressing himself on military matters, but his book covers more than its title suggests, and is particularly interesting because it contains a summary of the ideas and recommendations of many of his contemporary European engineers. Although he may have been a dilettante in military matters his opinions were nevertheless sufficiently respected by the experts for him to be invited to be a member of a royal commission on defence.

The most thorough, competent and all-embracing early book on fortification in the English language was written by Captain A. F. Lendy, a *Treatise on Fortification; or, Lectures delivered to Officers reading for the Staff* published in 1862. It shows that by mid-century British engineers were not only conversant with contemporary developments throughout Europe but were beginning to feel sufficiently confident to put forward recommendations in the field of coastal defence. These theories were the first really outstanding British contributions to the science of fortification since the construction of the Edwardian castles in Wales late in the thirteenth century.

Right
Fort Alexander at Koblenz

Far right
The fortification of Mainz, 1838

The years which followed the downfall of Napoleon and the settlement of the Congress of Vienna saw the establishment reasserting itself and the restoration of authority. The kingdom of Prussia formed the eastern and northern barrier to any expansionist threats from France, and the Germans were determined to entrench themselves with the utmost rapidity and the maximum vigour. After Vauban's demonstration of the superiority of attack over defence and Napoleon's rapid advances through Europe, a long cool look was needed at the potentialities of defence if the *status quo* was to be maintained against the ever-present threat of national and social revolution.

The strategic implications of a state of war were first contemplated in modern terms by Karl von Clausewitz, who in 1815 became chief of a Prussian army corps and later Gneisenau's chief of staff. His most important writings are contained in *Vomkrieg*, part of which is devoted to a consideration of the strategic value of fortresses. In the past wars had been limited by funds and the seasons. Now Clausewitz foresaw that huge standing armies would mow down opposition and fortresses would become no more than knots holding together a strategic web. Conscription had enabled France to raise a standing army of 732,000 in 1796.

There is no space to enumerate the 11 conditions Clausewitz specified as the functional reasons for the establishment of fortresses; briefly he pointed to their use as a secure depot for the vast arsenal and stores required by a modern army and their function as a tactical point of connection to secure the flank of an army in the field.

Feverish activity ensued in the towns which bordered the Rhine and the Danube. Koblenz was one of the first to prepare itself for an attack. It lay on the junction of the Rhine and the Moselle, with a population of about 12,000 and a garrison of about 11,000. Its main fortress had been destroyed by the French in 1799 and now its perimeter was enclosed behind a much larger enceinte, and the craggy, immensely strong fortress of Ehrenbreitstein was reconstructed to form the 'Gibraltar of the Rhine'. A new landfront was built on the hilltop above the river, consisting of a ravelin with a three-storey caponier designed as a strongly armoured outwork on the eastern flank. To the west the ground fell steeply to the river bank and needed no elaborate fortifications to make it invulnerable, but on the spur to the south another series of outworks dropped to a lower level culminating in Fort Helfenstein. Across the north front 40–50 guns could be brought to bear on any besieging artillery which came within range. The defensive guns were dug into casemates 12 metres deep and fired through tunnel-shaped embrasures.

Ehrenbreitstein, rebuilt between 1817 and 1828, was supported by other forts which ringed the town, of which Fort Alexander, modelled on the work of Montalembert, was the most notable. The fort was designed by General von Aster. The contemporary defences of many of the other German towns, like Cologne, Rastatt and Mainz, have now been demolished to make way for urban development. Mainz on the Rhine was a great army camp for 13,000 troops and about this time a new enceinte was thrown around the city by the Austrian general Scholl. It consisted of a tenaille front zigzagging in an arch across the river from bank to bank, with outlying forts, all built in the 1830s and designed to prevent a *coup de main*. Forts like Kreuz Schanze already showed the pattern which was to dictate the layout of so many of their successors throughout Europe. Fort Kreuz Schanze was an irregular polygon shaped like a detached bastion with strong caponiers placed in front and rear to cover its ditches. The plan of 1838 shows the approximate positions of the proposed adjoining forts which were to link up with the Hartenberg on the left to form an outer screen of detached forts some 500 metres in advance of the continuous town walls.

Farther up river lies Germersheim, its early nineteenth century fortifications almost intact. There the pattern was the same: an inner enceinte of Prussian fortifications depending for their strength upon massive multi-gun caponiers and an outer ring of detached forts. The defensive scheme was designed by Ritter von Schmauss and built in the 1840s. It was beautifully carried out in a combination of precise brickwork and rusticated masonry, the gates richly carved and ornamented.

The defences of Ingolstadt on the Rhine are even more extensive and impressive. The town is surrounded by parkland in which its fortifications still stand preserved. Ingolstadt was originally fortified by Daniele Speckle in 1575 and a contemporary model of the defences by Jakob Sandtner survives in the National Museum of Bavaria at Munich. It depicts a walled town buttressed with regularly spaced drum-towers, some of which remain. At the south and west corners stood mighty semi-circular bastions of steeply battered form so that they resembled truncated pyramids, their parapets pierced by embrasures. The new defences were designed by General Streider and built between 1828 and 1845. Undoubtedly Speckle influenced the new works. The town

CONTINUED ON PAGE 168

MDCCCXXXX

Left
The Ludwigstor at Germersheim, 1840

Below
Rear elevation of the gate

Side elevation of the Ludwigstor showing gun embrasures

Plan of Germersheim

163

A gun embrasure in the Ludwigstor

Ingolstadt: ravelin at the south end of the enceinte

Entrance to the south wall of the town

Left
Gun embrasures at Ingolstadt

Right
One of the oval forts on the south bank of the Danube

Below
Plan of Ingolstadt

Below right
The arc of a gateway through one of the keep cavaliers

Plan and section of a Maximilian tower at Linz

was surrounded by a line pierced at intervals by powerful U-shaped defensible barracks, their wings crowned with gun platforms and their fronts originally covered with counterguards. Between each pair of barracks stood a powerful caponier with its attendant works. At the junction with the Danube there was a large semi-circular-headed ravelin which seemed to follow the shape of Speckle's earlier bastion. The enceinte was surrounded by a wet ditch. On the other side of the river a great oval casemated work with projecting wings was the Réduit Tilly (1820) which formed a bridgehead supported on each side and in front by forts also oval and casemated. In the country beyond lay a series of detached works consisting of an inner ring of lunettes and small works and an outer ring of ten forts.

Austria under the rule of Metternich, the most conservative of the re-established states, set about putting its defences in order. Guarding Vienna from the west, Linz and Salzburg were to be refortified and, to prevent any penetration from Italy through the Tyrol, the famous 'quadrilateral' was formed, its sides resting on the rivers Mincio and Adige flanked by powerful fortresses at Peschiera and Mantua. Its base camp was formed by the fortified city of Verona. Farther up through the passes in the Alps lay isolated forts with the immensely powerful Franzenfeste barring the approach to the Brenner Pass.

The most novel and controversial works lay at Linz which was fortified by Prince Maximilian with 32 round towers, work on which commenced in 1830. Each tower was sunk into the ground and surrounded by a narrow ditch. The excavated material was used to form a glacis in front of the tower, the projection of whose surface lined up with the

crest of the parapet. There were three floors, including the basement, and embrasures covered the ditch. The gate at first floor level was approached by a drawbridge. The most significant features lay on the roof. Here 11 guns, mounted on newly modelled carriages so that they could be placed close together, could be laid so that their fire grazed the glacis in front. The guns were devised to enable all to be brought to bear on any given point at any time, their carriages being easily swung round on the inner circle of the tower. This was a great advance on earlier towers, such as those proposed by Montalembert where the lines of fire were governed by the angles of the embrasures and, in the event of a frontal attack, guns round the remaining three-quarters of the circle were forced to stand idle. It should be understood that the towers at Linz were designed to protect a military camp and to cover an army which would in turn support them. This germ of an idea developed into the entrenched camp of the late nineteenth century. Critics argued both for and against these circular towers. The Austrians used them again at Verona but they soon fell out of favour and most people, including the inhabitants of Linz, tended to refer to them as follies.

The fortifications of Verona were modernised by the Austrians in a series of beautifully executed commissions between 1830 and 1866. Before 1830 the Austrians had considered the Holy Alliance sufficient guarantee of their security, but the first of the liberal revolutions in France in that year caused them to reconsider the security of their possessions in Italy. The work on Verona was begun by the general of the Austrian engineers, Franz von Scholl, and completed by his successor Colonel Tunkler. The initial

project consisted of redesigning Sanmicheli's bastioned trace to the south and west of the fortifications north of the river which culminated in the castle of S Felice. Most of the original Renaissance trace had been destroyed in 1801 leaving only the Bastions of di Spagna and S Francesco intact. Perhaps out of respect for the great Italian architect these were retained with only minor modifications, but all the other bastions were rebuilt using accurately cut polygonal tufa. This type of construction characterises much of the Austrian engineers' work. The new bastions were built with detached walls and countersloping glacis as recommended by Carnot, having the advantage that musketeers could stand in the space between the walls and the ramparts to cover the ditch and the glacis. The salient angles of the bastions were crowned with small bastionettes to enfilade their faces. But von Scholl's trace must be considered as of secondary importance to his outer ring of detached forts built between 1832 and 1843. This heralded the concept of the entrenched camp, consisting in this case of outer forts capable of supporting each other behind which lay a continuous enceinte acting as an additional line of security for a mobile army of 120,000 men. The forts varied in shape, but many were polygonal, their four outer faces lined with casemates

and their gorges left open, protected only by muskets. In its centre each had a strong circular keep.

North of the city lies a high spur with precipitous cliffs. Its approaches were guarded by the city, with the castle of S Felice on the right flank and three detached forts on the left. On this ridge Scholl placed five circular forts modelled on those at Linz. They were later considered liable to be breached by enemy bombardment, but this would seem unlikely unless the enemy guns were well-concealed, as the forts on their elevated position had a fine view in all directions and were capable of pouring devastating fire on either side of the spur, whereas guns low down would have had little chance of retaliating. Everywhere the masonry is precise and tight fitting. It has resisted time and the obvious indifference of the Veronese. The walls are crisp and clean in spite of being neglected. The Austrian defences are vast, and Verona would certainly have been a tough nut to crack by the middle of the nineteenth century.

The Austrians were primarily interested in the possibility of an attack from the south-west. Wherever there is a well-placed hillock in the outer Alto Adige one finds a castle or a small fortress. Franzenfeste, now called Fortezza, straddles the valley looking south towards Italy, enclosing the defile of

An Austrian round tower at Verona

Far left
Interior of the Forte S Caterina at Verona

Left
An embrasure of the Forte S Caterina

Below left
*Austrian defences on the Bastione
S Spirito at Verona*

Below
The entrance to a round tower at Verona

Right
Franzenfeste; after Geographie Militaire

Far right
Gun embrasures guard the valley

An Austrian fort in the hills above Torbole

the Brixen Klause. Lying on the great post road from Verona to Innsbruck, it consisted of two distinct works joined by an underground passage and placed within musket shot of each other. The lower one, the main fort, was built on a granite rock in the centre of the valley, where the river, taking a sharp bend, forms a natural ditch 60 metres deep. The fortress was almost impregnable, holding a garrison of 1,200 men with three months' supply of food and water and ample additional resources in the form of reinforcements and running water at its back.

Coastal defence has often been a primary problem for the British. Edward I's castles were victualled from the sea, Bodiam was designed to counter French naval raids up a navigable river, Henry VIII's forts lined the foreshores of southern England, and the fort at Tilbury was built to prevent a repercussion of the alarming raid of the Dutch in 1667. A powerful naval nation would seem to have least need of coastal defences, but no fleet, however large, could be everywhere at once. Before the middle of the nineteenth century the disposition of the fleet was largely dictated by the direction of winds and, although the introduction of steam power gave it greater manoeuvrability, the advantage was largely offset by the need to patrol ever-increasing areas of the world's oceans to protect the outposts of the British Empire.

Up to the time of the Spanish Armada the use of hand to hand weapons had predominated and ships were designed primarily as mobile infantry platforms, but from about 1588 the gun became the main naval weapon. The one great advantage that ships had over shore defences was that they could swing round to bring a heavy broadside to bear and then make haste to move out of range of retaliation. The number and size of guns was gradually increased so that a ship of the line at the time of Nelson was capable of delivering a broadside of 50–60 guns. However ships suffered from three disadvantages. They were to some extent at the mercy of the weather, their rolling decks making accurate gunfire difficult, and the ships themselves were combustible. On the other hand coastal defence batteries fired from stable platforms, could be given bombproof protection, and their faces, which as targets were equivalent to the hulls of ships, could be constructed of durable materials such as brick, stone and later iron. Gradually more and more guns were introduced to a point when any vulnerable stretch of coast could be defended by multi-gun towers. This situation continued until a time when the advantages were slowly eroded by the intro-

Martello tower at Dymchurch in Kent

Below
A Martello tower; plan and section

Right
A section through one of the tours modèles

duction of shellfire and the application of steam as motive power for ships of war. Shell-firing guns were adopted by the French navy in 1837. Britain and America soon followed suit. Steam power began to be used about 1830. In 1841 the defences of Gibraltar were modified by the introduction of steamships. In 1843 the Americans launched their first screw warships and the Royal Navy followed with the commissioning of HMS *Dauntless* in 1844. The efficiency of the screw-driven ship was proved in the famous tug of war with a paddle steamer carried out in a Royal Navy test in 1845.

As naval gunnery improved, coast defence guns had to be supplemented by underwater obstacles. In 1805 Robert Fulton had shown that it was possible to destroy ships by detonating a charge against their hulls below the waterline. Gradually the number of guns in coast batteries dropped until in some instances at the end of the nineteenth century the British were using one-gun batteries.

During the Napoleonic Wars coastal defence theory was in its infancy and the European navies were still dominated by the large timber-hulled ships of the line. In 1783 two British frigates bombarded a tower on the coast of Corsica with no apparent effect. The following year *Fortitude* and *Juno* repeated the experiment without much impression. The round stone tower stood undamaged and her guns replying forced the British ships to haul off with a loss of 62 men and one ship fiercely on fire. Eventually the tower was forced to surrender through the bombardment of batteries landed on the shore firing redhot shot. The navy was so impressed by this defence that it failed to appreciate that a redoubt nearby had, with equal success, repulsed three British ships of the line. On naval advice the British govern-

ment, with the story of the defence of the Corsican tower still ringing in its ears, commissioned the construction of similar Martello towers along the coasts of Britain and the Channel Islands. These varied in design, but a typical one had a diameter of about 55 metres and a height of about 10 metres. A small door was approached by a drawbridge and guns were placed on the roof firing through merlons in the parapet, 3 metres thick. Although round towers did tend to deflect shot, the only main advantage that the Martello towers had over redoubts was the difficulty which would be experienced by any landing party in entering and capturing them. The project was commissioned in 1796 and various designs and sizes were produced, but circular towers were favoured. The siting of the Martello towers was decided upon after General Twiss's review of the defences of the south-east in 1803.

The French also feared landings on the coast. Montalembert in his project for the defence of Cherbourg in 1778 had advocated a ring of round and octagonal towers, and Napoleon's troops began to build *tours modèles* at vulnerable points along the French shore.

Two British strongholds were developed at this time which, if not primarily intended for coastal defence, had to consider the possibility of naval bombardment. Gibraltar had been annexed for Britain by Sir George Rooke in 1704 and had withstood three serious sieges in which enemy ships had unsuccessfully collaborated with forces trying to penetrate the defences of the landfront. Above the plain towered the North Front and in the rocky face deep casemates were excavated to provide overwhelming fire on the only ground of approach across which an attacking force could advance.

*Plan of Gibraltar in 1789; after
Drinkwater*

Two bastions flank the curtain of the castle at L'Aquila (photo Bramante Editrice)

Fort Regent on the island of Jersey; from a project of 1805

The British gunners had been so successful that Montalembert, on the raising of the siege in 1783, cited Gibraltar to support his theory in favour of the use of casemated artillery. Although the land approaches could be held without great difficulty, the sea defences of the town and the line of coast running to Europa Point needed a traditional fortified trace. King's Bastion, a fine masonry work with parapets 3 to 4·5 metres thick, was constructed in 1770 and Orange Bastion was built during the siege of 1779. In the ensuing years various reports were submitted for improving the defences and modernising the armament to counter the threat of screw-driven, and later iron-plated vessels. The report of 1859 described 'measures to be taken to place the fortress in a reasonable state of preparation to meet sudden attack from the sea'.

The only other important British fortress to be constructed in the early nineteenth century was at Jersey. Fort Regent was designed by Colonel John Humfrey to form the main stronghold of the island on Tower Hill above St Helier. It was part of a comprehensive scheme for the defence of Jersey which included new military roads and Martello towers along the coast. Fort Regent was begun in 1806 to prevent the recurrence of a French invasion which in 1781 had nearly captured the place. The fort was irregularly shaped, taking full advantage of the precipitous nature of the site. Its long flanks were guarded by bastions and the north and south approaches were each defended by two redans which joined at rather more than a right angle to form a tenaille front and which, through the introduction of flanks on their outer faces, became demi-bastions. This was a strange device, perhaps inspired by Montalembert whose influence can be seen in an unexecuted project for placing two round towers to defend an adjacent hilltop. The south front was covered by a counterguard, separated by a ditch from a long smooth glacis which sloped away to the south.

In 1794 the Americans, with their extended coastline and innumerable cities lying on or close to it, started to look to their defence. This young nation was soon to become, with Britain and Russia, one of the three most advanced exponents of the art of coastal defence. The early American forts were traditional, consisting of open works and earth parapets. Some had scarps revetted with timber and others had stone defences. Most followed the work of the French school of engineers. Fort McHenry guarding the approaches to Baltimore was typical. Built on the site of an earlier fort, it was constructed in 1794 as a 20 gun battery comprising a pentagonal fort with angle bastions, a ditch and covered way and a ravelin covering the entrance gate. An outer battery approximately following the south-east trace of the fort was added about 40 years later.

On the threat of another war with Britain new works were initiated in 1807 and American engineers began to adopt the ideas of Montalembert. The multi-gun fort constructed entirely of masonry with its guns housed in well-ventilated casemates, rising in several tiers somewhat resembling the broadside armament of a man of war, became the recognised method of defending the coast. Joseph G. Totten was appointed Chief Army Engineer in 1838, a post which he held until his death in 1864. He was instrumental in carrying out the recommendations of the Bernard Board which in 1821 had proposed an integrated national defence system for the harbours of the United States. Eighteen first class works and 32 smaller ones were planned, including open batteries and a few Martello towers. The large forts, like Sumter, Pulaski and Fort Jefferson in Florida could bring a concentration of fire which matched anything that a man of war could fire on to the fort. In the 1850s stone walls were reinforced with iron, and Totten was in the forefront, experimenting with an iron throat which could close across the mouth of an embrasure after its gun had fired. The Russians at Kronstadt soon introduced a system of iron laminates where bars 30 centimetres thick were tongued and grooved. And in 1861 the British introduced the 'Gibraltar shield' which could withstand the fire of 38 centimetre guns at 360 metres range. As will be seen, iron was to become one of the major materials in defensive works.

Fort Sumter in Charleston harbour was planned in the form of a pentagon, its salient angle to the front and each of its corners blunted to deflect shot. It was designed in 1827 and modified during construction so that on the outbreak of the Civil War it was uncompleted. When on 12 April 1861 Fort Sumter came under a murderous bombardment from Confederate batteries it was under-armed and unprepared for battle. It capitulated on the following day and passed into Confederate hands. Fort Sumter's major battle came two years later when it took on two ironclad ships in a 40 minute duel which ended in a victory for the fort, one ship being sunk and the remainder of the Union fleet withdrawing. The casemated guns were undamaged; the only ones that suffered being those in barbette positions on the terreplein. A determined siege then followed from land batteries supplemented by a naval attack at night which also failed. Fifteen

Fort McHenry (left) *and Fort Sumter*

*A 68-pounder gun: the last of the large
smoothbores, used at the time of the
Crimean War*

*Fieldworks protecting a mortar battery at
the siege of Sebastopol; after a drawing by
William Simpson, 1855*

Fort Pulaski; bird's eye view

inch shells were pumped into the fort until it became a mass
of ruins. In seven days it received 315 direct hits. This brave
defence showed that, with the muzzle-loading smoothbore
guns then available, a stone casemated fort was capable of
holding off the strongest naval attack and could resist for a
considerable period a land-based siege. The experience of the
Civil War shaped the plans of the future.

Fort Pulaski on the approaches to Savannah was a somewhat similar design. It was originally planned in 1827 as a
three tier fort, but the foundations proved too unstable to
support so massive a structure. Four years later the design
was modified and Robert E. Lee, then a young engineer
officer, was involved in its construction. Almost completed
by 1847, the fort was shaped in the form of a pentagon, its
faces and flanks consisting of one floor of casemates with guns
firing through embrasures and with barbette guns above on
the roof. The gorge was slightly recessed and contained the
barrack accommodation and the main gate, which was approached by a drawbridge from a ravelin. The ravelin replaced an earlier demi-lune whose halfmoon shape covered
the gorge, and the whole system was surrounded by a broad
moat.

The Crimean War had a profound effect on the development of coastal defences. In 1854 Franco-British forces
landed in the Crimea and slowly closed for the investment of
Sebastopol. The town was defended by a fortified trace at the
head of which stood the Malakoff, a large stone tower flanked
on either side by the Redan and the Little Redan. The coastline was held by a series of forts, started in 1783 and strengthened in 1834 by the addition of several coast forts and batteries, work on which was incomplete on the outbreak of war.

Fort Nicolas at Sebastopol; plan

The harbour entrance was sealed by sunken ships and General Todleben was appointed engineer in charge. Todleben's magnificent defence has been so well described as to need no amplification. The ingenuity with which he faced each fresh situation and the originality with which he fashioned the improvised earthworks, held in check the allied armies through the cruel winter of 1854. From the beginning the allies argued about the method of attack, the French preferring the slow methodical scientific approach they had learnt from Vauban, the British putting their faith in a sudden assault which on 18 June 1855 went in with disastrous effect and horrible loss.

The battle for the Russian coastal defences, though less well known, was equally important and the Russian fortifications, which proved so effective, later became models for British practice. The Franco-British fleet moved into the Black Sea and on 28 April 1854 arrived before Sebastopol to reconnoitre the defences. During the summer, in a lightning raid, two British ships had destroyed batteries at the mouth of the Danube, so that when, on 16 October, the fleet closed in for the attack, there was a feeling of confident expectation aboard the ships. The French attacked from the south and the British from the north, the inshore squadron closing to 660 metres to engage Fort Constantine. This was a powerful fort mounting over 100 heavy guns which soon got the range of the British ships. HMS *Queen* was quickly set on fire; *Rodney* grounded and had to be towed off, and several other ships were so badly damaged that they had to return to Malta for repairs. By evening, nothing achieved, the British squadron retired having lost 44 killed and 262 wounded.

No more naval attacks were undertaken against Sebastopol. The coastal forts had proved their worth.

The naval campaign in the Baltic had mixed results. On all fronts the war was bungled by aged commanders who had last seen active service in the Napoleonic Wars some 40 years earlier. The fleet, consisting of 28 ships of the line, many of them fitted with auxiliary screws, entered the Baltic and sailed for the great Russian naval base at Kronstadt. A careful reconnaissance soon revealed that the port was too strong to attack. Shore-based batteries were supplemented by a number of variously designed forts scattered across the open waterways. In addition to square and pentagonal designs, there existed round stone forts containing three tiers of casemated gun positions armed with heavy weapons. So the fleet departed in search of less suspecting prey. In August

Taking soundings under the Russian batteries off Kronstadt: in the background are three-decker forts; after Nolan

Right
Main fort on the island of Bomarsund;
plan

Below
Fort Nottick; plan and section

troops were landed on the Russian-held Åland Islands and an attack went in on Bomarsund. The Russian defences consisted of a semi-elliptical-shaped fort containing 62 casemates on each of two floors from which heavy guns mounted in the centre could sweep the bay almost at water level. Behind the ellipse, and part of the fort, stood a large horseshoe-shaped work on two floors with casemates armed with heavy guns to flank the landward approaches. In the hills behind lay three round towers, also casemated, their guns commanding the countryside. All the masonry was granite, constructed in polygonal form similar to the method used by the Austrians at Verona. Each tower had embrasures for 32 guns with loopholes between them for muskets. The vaults of the casemates were covered with two metres of sand and above that there was a timber roof shod with iron sheets to throw off the snow and to protect the timbers from hot shot and Congreve rockets. (William Congreve had begun experimenting with launchers in 1804, and his rockets soon developed an extreme range of 3,000 metres and were used successfully in the attack on Boulogne in 1806. Congreve himself must have been convinced from the start of their effectiveness for in 1805 he began experiments on applying armourplate to warships.)

Isolated and far from home, the Russian garrison did not put up much of a defence. Their embrasures proved vulnerable to accurate artillery which had been landed on the shore, and gunners in the main Russian work had difficulty in bringing more than six of their guns to bear on an attacking ship at any one time. But it was hardly a fair test of the capabilities of coastal defence for the allies knew that the forts had been constructed with shoddy workmanship.

In the following year a powerful fleet under the command of Admiral Dundas again sailed into the Baltic and prepared to bombard Sveaborg, the immensely strong fortress which barred the approach to Helsinki. The main fortress of Sveaborg had been built between 1749 and 1788, but it had been subsequently strengthened and rearmed by the Russians. Its five fortified islands presented an almost unbroken line of batteries. Although the allied naval losses were nominal, their bombardment, which continued through the night, did no more than destroy public buildings, for the fortress remained unsubdued, once again confirming the belief in the traditional superiority of forts over ships.

The American Civil War of 1861–65 threw up more ingenious innovations than almost any previous campaign. Both sides started ill-equipped and were forced to rely on their ingenuity. A number of devices emerged which were to reshape the conduct of war. The final destruction of Fort Sumter proved that masonry alone was incapable of withstanding the force of modern artillery. Muzzle velocity and accuracy were both increased by the introduction of rifling (its use with studded shot was being developed in 1842 by Colonel de Beaulieu in France) and by the explosive power of shells which had begun to replace solid shot in the French navy in 1837. Breech-loading, as opposed to muzzle-loading, was developed by Johann Dreyse and adopted by the Prussians in 1842, soon to revolutionise both the handling and the efficiency of big guns. Each year saw new developments and inventions which rapidly changed the face of war.

The Civil War also proved that, even though forts might easily withstand a naval bombardment, they were powerless to prevent a large fleet from penetrating any channel unless

Von Scheliha's Treatise on Coast Defence *illustrates the new underwater obstacles in use in 1868*

the defence was aided by underwater obstacles. With these obstacles in position and kept under fire from heavy batteries, no fleet could force a passage. The use of underwater obstacles is as old as naval warfare itself, but science and technology now stepped in to improve their efficiency. The torpedo and the mine were introduced in defence to supplement the use of sunken vessels, rocks, piles, booms and chains. The first large scale use of these devices occurred in the Civil War. The submarine mine, originally called a torpedo, could be fired in a number of ways, but the two most efficient methods caused it to explode either on contact with a ship or by remote electric detonation from an observation post on the coast.

The torpedo boat, later to be called the submarine, was invented during the war, and after a number of disastrous failures it successfully attacked in October 1863 one of the ironclad boats. Coast defences were supplemented later by torpedo rockets which could be fired, operated and detonated from the shore, and by the introduction of searchlights to illuminate a vulnerable channel. Electric beacons had been used in 1857 at South Foreland and in 1862 at Dungeness, and from these innovations there developed the concentrated and dispersed beams of the search and fixed lights used in defence.

In the second year of the American Civil War two iron ships fought out a thrilling duel. At the battle of Hampton Roads the ironclad *Merrimac* was engaged in pitched battle by the Union *Monitor*. Although the *Merrimac* had created havoc with the timber hulls of the Union fleet, its guns blazed ineffectually against the *Monitor* whose rotating turret* retaliated with equal lack of effect. The encounter, if

not conclusive, at least highlighted the remarkable properties of armourplating. Four years later the battle of Lissa clinched all arguments on the value of ironcladding when an Austrian squadron of ironclads practically annihilated a much larger contingent of Italian wooden-hulled ships.

The Crimean War held together an uneasy alliance between Britain and France. The peace which followed was apprehensive as Britain watched the French navy being built up, equipped with the latest technical devices and armed with the new screw-driven ships, their hulls sheathed in iron. The bombardment of Kilburn at the mouth of the Dnieper in 1855 by three French floating batteries, which emerged unscathed after a four hours' engagement during which the French ships were hit repeatedly, proved conclusively the value of armourplating. To make matters worse for the British the French began to equip a great naval arsenal at Cherbourg, menacing the English south coast ports, and ringed it with a formidable defensive screen. By 1858 Britain, her navy largely dispersed at overseas stations and her home defences hardly touched for over 100 years, stood in peril of invasion. It is still unknown whether the threat of a sudden attack was serious, but Palmerston feared that the two countries might inadvertently become involved in a state of war. In December 1858 a committee, set up to investigate the relative strengths of the French and British navies revealed the frightening fact that France already had superiority of capital ships in the Channel. Immediately steps were taken

* In 1860 Captain Cowper Coles, RN, had written a paper advocating the use of revolving gun turrets. Later they became all-important in naval architecture.

in an attempt to safeguard the main British naval arsenals and deep water anchorages to which a fleet might have to withdraw to rearm and repair the scars of battle. It was to be an expensive undertaking, unpopular with Parliament and criticised by those who believed that the Royal Navy formed an impenetrable shield for the defence of Britain.

The Royal Defence Commission report came out in 1860 with recommendations for works at the royal dockyards of Portsmouth, Plymouth, Pembroke and Chatham, plus protection for the harbours at Portland, Dover and Cork. Work had already begun on some schemes when the government axed the recommended expenditure from £10,350,000 to £6,570,000. As the work progressed costs inevitably rose. In some cases foundations proved to be more expensive than anticipated, new heavy guns cost more and the considerable use of iron-plating was expensive. The price of labour and materials rose and the commission of 1861 recommended an improvement in barrack accommodation. Higher standards of ventilation, drainage and water supply were called for, while space allocated for each soldier was to be increased from 37 square metres to at least 56. Only after considerable opposition did the government get its way and the *Fortifications Act* was passed in 1867. Work was already well under way at all the main naval ports.

The defences consisted of three types each with its own distinctive characteristics. Coastal defence forts were constructed close to the shore. They were modelled on Russian designs in the Crimea, each irregularly shaped in the form of a long hooked arm with casemated batteries. Built some distance away, the barrack accommodation usually consisted of a large defensible horseshoe. Secondly, there were forts built in the sea. The British had already experimented at Fort Perch Rock, built at the entrance to the river Mersey between 1826 and 1829 to the designs of Captain Kitson. Except at low tide this fort is surrounded by seawater. But most of the new forts were placed in mid-channel, multi-gun circular structures modelled on the Russians' work in Kronstadt harbour. The third type of defence consisted of detached forts forming elements in a major fortress and strongly influenced by Montalembert. These were intended to repel an army which had landed somewhere down the coast and was now circling to attack the port from the rear. Each landfort was to be supported by neighbours. Of the 76 forts in course of construction or completed by 1867 19 were land forts and the remainder either coastal defence forts or sea forts.

The report on the sea defences of Milford Haven was published in 1858 and work began immediately to safeguard the great anchorage at the head of which lay the naval dockyard of Pembroke. In addition to forts placed in the sea, there were three major coastal forts with barracks widely separated from the gun positions. Fort Hubberstone was ready to receive her armament in 1860 but, because modifications were carried out to provide iron shields, she was not completed until 1863 at a cost of £73,600. The battery lay on the cliff edge four miles from the dockyard and originally consisted of 12 casemates, later supplemented by barbette positions on the roof. A horseshoe-shaped barrack block placed on the crest of the hill secured the rear of the gun positions, and beyond the barracks lay a dry ditch defended from its counterscarp by granite galleries placed to flank the ditch. The barrack block was modified during construction to pro-

Fort Perch Rock at the entrance to the Mersey

Left
Fort Hubberstone guarding Milford Haven

Below
Counterguard galleries flanking the ditch at Fort Hubberstone

Right
The west battlements at Fort Popton before alterations

Below right
The old gun emplacements at Fort Popton, Milford Haven

Design for a fort at Spithead with 49 guns in two tiers and ten guns in revolving turrets, the whole of the exterior clad in iron; after Jervois

vide bombproof accommodation and was not completed until 1865. This type of fort was never intended to withstand a full scale siege but should have been capable of resisting a sudden assault by enemy marines landed on the coast.

Sea forts were a different proposition. They depended for their defence upon unscaleable walls rising sheer from the water's edge. Stack Rock (1859–61) at Milford Haven was the least successful as it was built on a rocky outcrop which might under certain circumstances have provided a tenuous foothold for an attack. All four forts in the Solent guarding the approach to Portsmouth are round structures rising directly from the sea. They are partly clad with iron, although they were at one time intended to be fully sheathed with this material. The Solent forts were begun in 1863 against considerable opposition originating mainly from those who wished to put their whole trust in the navy and its deployment of floating batteries. But those who advocated the sea forts carried the day and the forts were built at great expense caused largely by foundation difficulties. The largest one was completed in 1880 having cost over £242,000, a sum which might be compared with the more meagre cost of the coast defence forts at Milford Haven, the most expensive of which was Fort Popton at £75,600 and the cheapest, South Hook Fort, costing £44,000.

First Portsmouth, then Plymouth and Chatham in the 1870s were ringed by detached forts. At Portsmouth a group of forts, of which Fort Brockhurst is the best preserved, were built to cover the approach to Gosport. Fort Brockhurst (1858–62) consisted of a polygonal fort with casemates from which guns could fire directly across the countryside. It was surrounded by a wet ditch, flanked by three caponiers, the

The 100-ton gun in the battery at Fort Rinella, Malta

Spitbank fort guarding Portsmouth

central one being a powerful work of the type advocated by Montalembert and currently being used by the Prussians. The gorge wall was pierced for musketry defence, and in its centre stood a circular keep armed with artillery in casemates and with a series of small bastions from which muskets could flank the ditch.

Behind Portsmouth lies the Portsdown hill, its crest providing a remarkable panorama of the naval port and the surrounding countryside. An enemy in possession of this hill could have pounded the naval installations into a mass of rubble. To foil him four large forts and three minor works were constructed, the last and the most ambitious land fortification project to be built in Britain. Fort Wallington was typical, its guns firing from barbette positions on earth

ramparts supplemented by a mortar battery at the northern angle. The fort was designed in the shape of a polygon surrounded by a dry ditch flanked by caponiers firing in one direction and a two-storey counterscarp gallery which covered the two northern arms of the ditch. The barracks were in the gorge, situated in a tall brick structure loopholed for musketry defence with a large loopholed redan projecting in the direction of the town. Fort Wallington, started in 1861, was completed in 1874 at a total cost of just over £100,000.

Although never tested in war, there can be no doubt that the forts were as advanced as anything on the continent and by this time British engineers like Burgoyne, Jervois and Lefroy were fully aware of the changing nature of warfare and its implications for permanent fortification.

Above
Fort Brockhurst at Portsmouth

Above right
Plan of one of the forts in the Gosport lines, Portsmouth; after Lendy

Right
Plan and section of the circular keep at Fort Brockhurst; after Lendy

*Casemates for the big muzzle-loading guns
at Fort Delimara, Malta*

*Overleaf left
The ditch and a counterscarp gallery at
Fort Delimara*

*Overleaf right
One of the 38-ton RML guns at Fort
Delimara*

Sliema Point Battery at Malta

Bottom
*Interior of a British casemate at Fort St
Lucian, Malta*

With the extension of imperial power Britain's defence commitments stretched across the world. By 1856 she had major military responsibilities in Gibraltar, Malta, Corfu, Bermuda and Mauritius, with lesser liabilities at St Helena and Ascension Island. India, Canada, the West Indies, the Cape of Good Hope, Ceylon and Australia, whilst requiring defensive measures, were capable of financing them from their own resources. The task of defending the British Empire was a prodigious one. Discounting the 100,000 troops required for the defence of Britain, of which 27,000 were needed in Ireland, and the fairly heavy requirements for the defence of the Channel Islands, the main emphasis in imperial defence fell upon Gibraltar and Malta. There is no better place than Malta to study the changing pattern of permanent fortification from the time of the resumption of control by Britain in 1800 to the outbreak of the First World War. At first the army was overawed by the prodigious expanse of the fortifications inherited from the Knights of St John. Mile upon mile of yellow limestone bastions and curtains seemed to stretch into the distance and the sheer task of manning them, let alone modifying them, daunted the British. Up to the 1860s the task lay mainly in modernising the armament and improving barrack accommodation, but in 1871 the army began a new continuous line to cover the landward approach to the naval dockyard. From then on there was an unbroken policy of modernisation and new building as more and more coastal forts sprang up in defence of the Island. With the opening of the Suez Canal in 1869 the pace quickened and the tendency was towards providing forts with no more than four or five large guns, at first housed in casemates and after 1878 mounted in the open, *en barbette*. Gradually there was a

Right
The keep at Fort Musta in the Victoria lines, Malta

Far right
A gun emplacement at Fort Musta designed to minimise the chance of shot entering the fort

Proposed design of Fort Tombrell, Malta; plan

separation of the observation position from the gun position made possible by the introduction of field telephones. Colonel Watkin invented a position finder so that guns could be laid and fired by electricity from a distant position finder station.

The diversity of design in the British forts in Malta is amazing, hardly any two are alike. The early ones, like Sliema Point Battery (1872–76) are erect and richly decorated with carved gothic motifs like some medieval fortress. The plan is fanshaped with four casemates for 25 and 38 ton muzzle-loading guns. Begun in 1876, Fort Delimara followed an irregular site on a promontory overlooking the great bay of Marsaxlokk. The deep dry ditch with vertical scarp and counterscarp walls was flanked by counterscarp galleries and the guns, six heavy 38 ton rifled muzzle-loaders, still surviving but badly rusted, were dug into large casemates in the cliff face. But already at that time the value of casemated guns was in dispute. After the battle of Duppel in 1864 the Prussians decided that embrasures were useless. In the same year the British developed the Moncrief mounting, the first of a long line of devices which allowed the barrel of a gun to project above the parapet for firing and to recoil to a point of safety concealed behind the thickness of the parapet. Eight years later designs were submitted for Fort Tombrell in Malta, with a regular hexagonal trace mounting six 64-pounder RML guns on Moncrief carriages, protected in the rear by a large traverse which ran the width of the fort. In front of the traverse and facing out to sea stood three 11-inch guns in barbette mountings. In those early days of the development of technology it was only possible to mount comparatively light guns on disappearing carriages, although gradually the techniques were improved to allow the utilisation of much heavier guns.

As the range of guns increased the early land defences of Malta became outdated. The old Floriana and Cottonera Lines were too near the heart of the naval dockyard to be practicable and in 1866 a recommendation was made to build a line of five ring-forts to form a large semi-circle around the capital and the port. However the rate of improvement in gun design was so rapid that hardly had this recommendation been made than it was outdated. In that very year the French army decided to adopt Chassipot's greatly improved breech-loading gun and in the following year Krupps exhibited a 50-ton breech-loader capable of firing a 1,000 lb. shell. At the same time Britain was experi-

Above left
Fort S Leonardo in Malta ; plan

Above
*The 100-ton gun battery at Fort Rinella,
Malta ; plan*

The ditch of Fort Leonardo from the scarp

Wolseley Battery, Malta; plan

menting with coiled barrels which greatly increased muzzle velocity and thus range. So in Malta the first plan was abandoned, and in 1873 the Victoria Lines were projected on an escarpment much farther to the north. There half a dozen new forts and casemated batteries were joined by a continuous line of infantry positions.

Meanwhile work on the coastal forts forged ahead. Fort St Leonardo was completed in 1878 on a triangular plan with barbette guns firing out to sea along one face of the triangle, and a strong keep, completely detached from the rest of the fort by a moat, was placed in the opposite angle. On the landward side the fort was protected by a spur, at that date still a favourite device of British engineers, its long pointed shape stretching back like a tail from the fort.

Between then and the outbreak of the First World War some dozen new forts were constructed on the island and many of the earlier ones like Fort Delimara converted to take large breech-loading guns and quick-firing guns on barbette mountings as the old muzzle-loaders were gradually phased out. Britain had pioneered the introduction of breech-loading guns but, after some failures, had reverted to the old muzzle-loaders. In 1882 she changed back to breech-loading guns. 9·2-inch BL guns were placed in the open

above the casemates which in places had to be strengthened to take the load. Fort Delimara was re-equipped in 1888.

Of the new forts in Malta, at least two types show significant development. In the last decades of the nineteenth century Britain was still experimenting with larger and larger muzzle-loading guns. In 1875 an 80-ton gun had been completed at the arsenal at Woolwich, to be followed soon by the 100-ton gun with a calibre of 17·72 inches. The Italians had ordered these giant weapons to be fitted to their newest battleships and the British suddenly became apprehensive of the possibility of the Italian navy standing outside the maximum range of the guns of Malta and Gibraltar and bombarding the naval installations with impunity. A decision was taken to despatch three of these weapons to the Mediterranean bases. In each case a new fort was designed to house just one gun. In 1884 Fort Rinella was completed in Malta and the heavy gun landed in the harbour to be hauled with considerable difficulty up the tortuous road into its position in the fort. Like its sister guns at Fort Cambridge in Malta and Napier of Magdala Battery in Gibraltar, it was never fired in anger, but it gave the authorities considerable anxiety. These were the only guns of the British army which could not be laid by hand,

The 100-ton gun at Napier of Magdala Battery, Gibraltar; after Inglis

*An 8-inch BL gun on a hydro-pneumatic
mounting, in its loading position*

Below
*The same gun raised in the firing position;
after Sydenham Clarke*

traversing, elevating and depressing being carried out by steam power. Maybe the British need not have worried for the end of the big muzzle-loading guns was in sight. After all that effort to ship them out and haul them into position, their possible opponent, the 100-ton gun on the Italian battleship *Duilio*, blew up.

The final development of the fort lay in the substitution of the Twydall Profile for the traditional ditch flanked from caponiers or counterscarp galleries. A good illustration is Wolseley Battery, built between 1897 and 1899 to mount four 6-inch quick-firing guns. The ground in front of the barbette mountings sloped gently forward to terminate in a shallow scooped out arc which embraced the whole front of the gun positions. This depressed area was filled with loose barbed wire and its outer edge secured by a barbed wire fence. Except for the entrance gate the back of the fort was defended by a spiky steel palisade three metres high. In this design flanking fire was completely abolished and the defence of the fort depended on frontal fire from rifles, which could quickly be reloaded, and from machine-guns. The British army had adopted the Martini-Henry rifle in 1871; Hiram Maxim invented the belt-loading machine-gun in 1883, and the British introduced the Vickers-Maxim machine-gun in 1891. Barbed wired obstacles and rapid fire from small arms were to re-establish the superiority of defence, a superiority which culminated in the stagnation of trench warfare in the First World War.

Gradually the gun as a defensive factor began to assume greater importance than the bricks and mortar of the fortifications which housed it. The casemate was abandoned, its

position unsurped by two diametrically opposed systems. On the one hand there was the growing popularity of the open gun position, especially in coastal defence work, helped by the introduction of smokeless gunpowder by the French in 1884. And at the other extreme lay the development of the armoured cupola with the gun and its mechanisms sunk deep into the earth. In coast defence work large puffs of smoke no longer revealed the exact positions of the guns, which were dispersed, being laid and fired electrically from a position finder station. At first the disappearing gun was popular, the barrel sometimes sliding below an overhead metal shield providing some protection for the gunners, but with the introduction of effective breech-loading guns (Britain began to use them after about 1882) it was possible to use high-angled rifled ordnance. The guns placed behind the con-

A revolving armoured cupola operated by hand; after Hennebert

tinuous parapet on a cliff were completely obscured from any attacking ships. Not only did the guns develop greater accuracy after 1855 but gradually their range was extended. With the introduction of the magazine rifle forts could be more easily defended and in any case there was less likelihood of their being attacked by landing parties because warships in the later nineteenth century before the introduction of assault craft had little space to spare for landing parties.

In America the Endicott Board, formed in 1885, shifted the emphasis from the structure of the fort to the weapons contained within it. Forts became simple low-lying structures in reinforced concrete blending with the countryside. Earlier the guns of a fort had cost anything between a sixth and a tenth of the total cost, now they began to assume three-quarters of the overall cost of a fort. Their numbers

were also reduced (the days of the multi-gun fort were over) and by 1906 the United States was also installing single gun batteries in some of her overseas possessions.

British military engineers like Sydenham Clarke, O'Callaghan, J. F. Lewis, B. R. Ward and E. R. Kenyon began to take an active interest in continental developments, visiting the armament manufacturers and whenever possible the sites of military installations. For in Europe the stage was being set for the last great demonstration of the defensive power of permanent fortifications. Old faiths were rudely shaken as the technocrat usurped the position of authority previously held by the geometrician.

The armoured cupola now began to attract the attention of military planners. It was immensely expensive and under certain conditions of attack its occupants could be momen-

A Chatillon and Commentary disappearing gun turret in the raised position; from Clarke's Reports

tarily blinded. Being encased in this shell of iron, sandwiched between the sharp edges of an exploding gun and the dripping surfaces of the outer skin where the condensation ran down in rivulets, the psychological effect cannot have been healthy. But in the event of bombardment, the protection afforded by the dome of iron formed a powerful compensation for the claustrophobic conditions. There were many solutions. Mougin invented a cupola with a completely new system of fortification. His fort consisted of huge blocks of concrete buried deep in the earth from which rose three cupolas each manned with two 150-millimetre guns. Supporting these and providing close defence were four disappearing machine-gun cupolas supplemented by observation domes and all the paraphernalia of forced ventilation and electric lighting. The entrance was covered by an

A disappearing searchlight cupola; after Cramwinckel

armourplate which could be raised and lowered by an hydraulic ramp and from there the path into the fort twisted and turned like those in an ancient Greek fortress, so that the enemy on penetrating the structure would be caught at a number of right-angled turns. The ditch was now abolished and the machine-gun, firing 700 rounds a minute, was intended to keep enemy infantry at a distance. Around the outside of the fort ran a railway track so that trucks carrying guns, which could be raised by hydropneumatic power, could be moved forward and withdrawn as the tactical situation required: an ingenious method and a strong pointer to future developments.

In 1887 Colonel Voorduin of the Dutch corps of engineers produced a simple fort consisting of a low mass of concrete from which projected iron cupolas housing twin guns. The ends of the concrete contained caponiers from which guns fired across the intervening space between forts, and the scheme had the merit of being cheap because its trace was comparatively short and enclosed very little interior space. In early forts the need had been to provide sufficient interior space for a comparatively large garrison cumbrously to man inefficient cannon. With the introduction of quick-firing guns and pre-prepared shell and cartridge ammunition the garrison could be drastically reduced.

The munition factories of Europe advertised their wares and their products were sold to anyone prepared to pay. For example, Colonel Schumann's armoured front was built into the Sereth Line in Rumania between 1889 and 1892. Germany and France produced the goods and, rather pathetically, the most avid purchaser was little Belgium.

The Franco-Prussian War of 1870 saw France ill-prepared to withstand the assault of determined well-trained troops. Leaving isolated outposts of resistance the French fell back on the capital which was protected by a circuit of detached forts forming a perimeter of nearly 48 kilometres, its design still conforming to the bastioned trace rationalised by Vauban 200 years earlier. Fort Issy was a typical example of a conservative French attitude to defence. Dating from the 1840s when one school of French thought wanted to bastion Paris with a complete enceinte some ten miles out from its centre, only the sheer scale and expense of the undertaking prevented its implementation. So detached forts like Issy were built. Sydenham Clarke described it as a fort built on a traditional bastion trace mounting 60 guns, 'which may have flanked everything flankable, but were utterly unable

Left
Section through an underground fort designed by Mougin; after Sydenham Clarke

Right
Fort Issy defending Paris; plan

Redoubt des Hautes Bruyères at Paris; plan

Right
*Trace of Brialmont's enceinte at Antwerp;
after Lewis*

*Fort de Broechem, one of the ring forts of
Antwerp*

to cope with siege batteries, on which a mere fraction of them could be brought to bear'. Fortunately for the French they were quick to learn, and as the siege of Paris materialised they threw up polygonal redoubts which were modelled on current German practice. The Redoubt des Hautes Bruyères was an efficient solution to the problem. The guns still fired through embrasures, their flanks protected by traverses, but the ramparts were of earth and the ditch enfiladed from caponiers. If it did nothing else for the French, the Franco-Prussian War shook the dust from the higher echelons of the French command and tolled the death knell of the bastioned trace.

Of all the great ring-fortresses of western Europe, Antwerp was the mightiest; yet when put to the test it was one of the least successful. It was designed to be a base for operations, a refuge for the government and a réduit for national survival. At various times four lines of defence had been built at Antwerp. The Duke of Wellington supervised the construction of the old enceinte between 1815 and 1818 and its citadel, defended by General Chassé, bravely withstood a two years' siege in 1830. By 1859 its bastions and curtains were thoroughly outmoded and were dismantled. In that year Henri Brialmont (1821–1903), the most noteworthy of the Belgian engineers, was called in to design a continuous new enceinte with, four kilometres farther out, a string of eight detached polygonal forts, to which four more were later added, making Antwerp the most powerful fortress of its day. Brialmont's trace was complex but its defensive power hinged on the use of large pointed caponiers armed with many guns, becoming forts in their own right, faced by a complex ravelin and backed by a short curtain in the middle of which stood a rectangular block of defensible barracks. As time passed even this extensive defence system was not considered adequate to safeguard the town and between 1878 and 1898, five new ring-forts were built some 9·5 to 14 kilometres farther out. Thus the circumference of forts was extended from a mere 43 kilometres in the case of Brialmont's forts to an enormous perimeter of 106 kilometres for the ring forts. The Belgians went on adding more and more forts to close the gaps, but, as quickly as they built, the problem changed. With the development of mighty new mobile howitzers (the Russians were using one with a calibre of 280 millimetres in 1912) the ancient 150-millimetre guns in the forts were sadly outmatched. All the forts had been clearly marked on innumerable drawings. Their silhouettes were plainly visible and their structures could not be moved, so that every German gunnery officer had the location of each one pinpointed on his maps. Their fate was inevitable. The turn of the century saw the Belgians moving their heavy guns from the forts and deploying their effective artillery in the intervals. The position was thus reversed. Instead of the forts being strongpoints in the line of battle, supported by a field army, they were utilised to provide flanking fire for the guns in the intervals. Some forts were equipped with traditore, that is with guns facing only to the flanks and the rear in order to sweep the intervals.

When the First World War began and German troops flooded into Belgium many of the Antwerp forts were unfinished. Some lacked cupolas and most had old guns firing black powder and only effective over short ranges. The forts too were badly ventilated and their interiors soon filled with

Below
Plan and section of a Liège fort

Right
The ditch of Fort Lonçin at Liège

Overleaf
An armoured cupola at Fort Lonçin

the poisonous fumes from their own guns and from the German shells which burst upon them causing fissures in the concrete. The concrete was poor and soon broke under the bombardment of General von Beseler's heavy Skoda and Krupp siege artillery. The Belgian troops on seeing so many of their cherished forts collapse before their eyes were soon dispirited. On 14 August 1914 the Belgian government withdrew to the city. Its bombardment lasted 11 days and its surrender followed. So collapsed the greatest of the ring-fortresses. But it was not alone. Liège and Namur were similarly defended and shared a similar fate. Liège was surrounded by 12 forts, the best work of Brialmont. They were built in the 1880s to a uniform plan and originally designed to withstand a pounding from 21-centimetre guns. It is hardly surprising that they crumbled a quarter of a century later to the mighty 42-centimetre howitzers rapidly brought up by the Germans. The Liège forts were triangular, surrounded by a dry ditch protected by counterscarp galleries in the angles of the triangle. The rear side of the triangle was recessed into a bastion trace with a short central curtain and through this lay the gate. The triangular fort, including the scarp wall, was built of earth into which were sunk deep concrete magazines, barracks and gun positions so that the only things that protruded above the level of the ground were the iron cupolas with howitzers in the middle and the rear, and quick-firing guns with a searchlight and observation cupola in front. The forts lay between five and six kilometres from the city centre and were spaced about four kilometres apart. Fort Lonçin is preserved as a national monument for it was there that in 1914, under heavy bom-

CONTINUED ON PAGE 217

Left
An observation cupola at Fort de Vaux

Right
Plan of Fort de Vaux at Verdun as reconstructed just before the First World War

Inside a gallery in the underground fort

bardment, the fort's magazine blew up, ripping out the iron cupolas like so much waste paper and slaughtering many of the gunners.

By the beginning of 1914 the reputation of permanent fortifications had suffered such a severe blow that it seemed unlikely that anyone would in future trust his defence to them and, had it not been for one fortress, this would probably have been the end of the line. As it turned out Verdun in 1916 was a very different proposition for the German army.

Verdun is an ancient city and has seen many sieges. Its second citadel was designed by Vauban. Its detached forts were erected in 1874 by Brialmont to form part of the general defensive curtain devised by General Séré de Rivières for the protection of the French frontier. Most of the forts were pentagonal with ditches filled with barbed wire and protected from caponiers. Although their construction was excellent the French were worried about the ability of the forts to withstand heavy bombardment and in 1888 tested Fort Malmaison to destruction. As a result they modified the designs, replacing or facing masonry with reinforced concrete so that when war broke out forts like Douaumont had a covering of one metre of reinforced concrete separated from the main structure by one metre of sand. This fort, which was trapezoidal in shape, mounted twin 55-millimetre guns in a salient angle and two single 155-millimetre guns on the flanks set in iron cupolas which were raised for firing by counterweights. Close defence depended upon two outer belts of barbed wire with wire and railings in the ditch covered by machine guns. However with the fall of the Belgian forts the French army lost confidence in the ability of the Verdun forts to withstand a German advance and withdrew from them nearly all their main armour, with the result that when, on 21 February 1916, they faced a massive German bombardment from 'Big Berthas', the great 42-centimetre German howitzers, the forts were hardly equipped to reply. Instructions were muddled and Fort Douaumont fell to a small party of Germans with hardly a shot being fired. Then almost overnight the situation changed. General Pétain issued his famous order, 'They shall not pass'. The remaining advanced forts were pounded into a mass of rubble and mud yet strangely they did not collapse and the troops were able to survive deep in the concrete dugouts. The 42-centimetre shells, whose shock in ordinary ground penetrated to a depth of 14 metres, now hit the mass of concrete and its cushion of sand without appreciable impression. The forts were well-ventilated by filtered air drawn in under slight pressure from some distance away and life was able to continue.

'France must be regarded as a great fortress,' wrote Schlieffen. With the jagged peaks of the Alps to the south, the defences ran north from the great fortress of Belfort through the high hills of the Ballon to Epinal, Toul and Verdun, the gaps in the passes filled with barrier forts. Then to the north the country was studded with powerful fortresses. The Dutch, like the Belgians, feared more that their country might lie in the path of the great right hook which the German army would be forced to take to outflank the fortresses in any attempt to break in upon the French capital, than by the fear of direct invasion for the purposes of occupation. Holland had an ally, water, but not all the Dutch provinces were low-lying and capable of being flooded. In the late 1860s a plan was evolved to cut off from attack the major cities of the country. From the old fortified town of Heusden, lying to the north-east of Amsterdam close to the waters of Zuiderzee, a line of forts and water obstacles was to be drawn to Utrecht, acting as a pivot, and beyond to the broad rivers which snake to the sea across the lowlands of southern Holland. This was the New Water Line. Two of the largest works covered the approaches to Utrecht. Fort Rhijnauwen was begun in 1868 and Fort Vij Vechten in the following year. Their construction continued until about 1880.

Fort Rhijnauwen was a lopsided pentagon surrounded by a broad ditch of placid water some 6–8 metres deep and about 50 metres wide. Its front was protected by a powerful caponier completely surrounded by the ditch and at its rear, in the middle of the gorge, stood a powerful keep, or last

Plan of Fort Rhijnauwen outside Utrecht

*Loopholes in the caponier and the wet ditch
at Fort Rhijnauwen*

Entrance to the keep-reduit at Rhijnauwen

Loopholes inside the central gallery of the keep-reduit

stronghold, also pentagonal in shape with boldly projecting brick caponiers on each corner. The advanced faces of the fort were terminated at their extremes by projecting caponiers and by flanks with orillions close to the main caponier. The guns were everywhere placed in barbette positions on the terreplein up to which they were hauled along shallow ramps. As usual in Holland, the standard of the brickwork is superb. Fort Vij Vechten was both more complex and more traditional. The same type of wet ditch surrounded the fort

and the keep occupied the gorge, standing on its own small glacis resembling a stunted Norman motte. But the trace consisted of broad bastions with blunted angles.

Brialmont had been strongly in favour of the last stand keep, but later opinion was divided. Some maintained that the keep stiffened resistance and allowed the garrison to withdraw to a position from which it might later sally out and recapture the major work. Others thought it encouraged the idea of retreat.

Fort Vij Vechten at Utrecht; plan

Left
The underground barracks at Fort Vij Vechten

Right
Gun embrasure in the keep-reduit

Left
Loopholes in the rear of the barrack block covering the ditch of Fort de Queuleu

Right
An underground passage leading to the infantry parapets

Below right
A French fort with guns on a cavalier, sited independently of the trace and protected by traverses: in front is a low parapet for infantry: the ditches are defended by caponiers; after Hennebert

Fort de Queuleu at Metz; plan

In the area around Strasbourg and Metz the Germans developed their most advanced thinking on fortification in the era between the Franco-Prussian War and the outbreak of the First World War in 1914. Three examples will trace this evolution. Guarding Metz in the year 1869, Fort de Queuleu is the first. It was started by the French and considerably modified by the Germans so that it consisted of a pentagonal bastion trace with masonry scarp and counterscarp walls, but the whole of the terreplein was raised as an immense earthen cavalier armed with guns for distant defence only. The only significant difference in the main French forts constructed after the war of 1870 lay in the fact that the guns no longer lined the parapets of the bastion trace, but were pulled back and grouped on the large cavalier. The bastion trace no longer fulfilled its flanking function. The ditch of

Fort Queuleu was flanked by counterscarp galleries beyond which were dug countermines. The gorge and the landward face of the bastions were occupied by barracks which, although loopholed on the flanks, look remarkably vulnerable to an attack from the rear. The fort was essentially somewhat conservative.

By 1893 the defensive situation had changed and the Germans, however reluctant they might have been to think in terms of fixed defences, were using their ingenuity. The new works lay at Muttzig-Molsheim on a hill not far from Strasbourg. Schlieffen had himself suggested fortifying this area, remarking 'however much it goes against our tradition to build fortifications, we cannot, as the weaker side, reject the means used by our opponent to paralyse our military plans'.

225

Iron railings on the counterscarp at Fort Blotten

Fort Blotten at Mutzig-Molsheim; plan

At Molsheim the influence of Brialmont is apparent. Fort Kaiser Wilhelm II and Fort Blotten were both designed in the form of an equilateral triangle. The forts were surrounded by dry ditches with vertical masonry scarps and counterscarps, the ditches being covered from counterscarp galleries in the points of the triangles. There was no covered way, but instead a high spiky iron fence enclosed the perimeter, resting on and secured to the crest of the counterscarp wall. The middle of the triangle consisted of a compact mass of earth and concrete with four shallow-domed iron cupolas carrying the main armament of 38-centimetre howitzers in rotating turrets. Round the main armament were six quick-firing guns similarly designed but for use in close defence, and at the corners of the triangle there were iron-armoured lookouts.

The Molsheim forts were built between 1893 and 1899, after which their surroundings were slowly modified. They show in embryonic form the group or feste principle of defence which was to become the most notable German contribution to permanent fortifications. The main forts mutually supported each other, but there were other batteries scattered across the hillside, the whole top of which was taken over and strung round with barbed wire emplace-

An iron door seals the counterscarp gallery

Two of the four 6-inch howitzer cupolas
at Fort Blotten

Muzzle of a howitzer

Below
*Plan of a German feste, fortified Group
Guentrange (Fort Ober-Gentringen) at
Thionville*

ments. Barracks and infantry trenches were woven into the
pattern of mutual defence.

The fully developed German feste was initiated about 1900
in the area around Metz and Thionville. Each group occupied a large area, and there were three around Thionville:
feste Ober-Gentingen (1899–1909), now given the French
name of Fort de Guentrange, the feste at D'Illange (1903)
and the fortified group Koenigsmacker (1908–13) forming a
triangle of defence around the town.

Each occupied a large irregular area on a hilltop, surrounded by a broad ditch, in places deep and elsewhere

Top right
An underground diesel engine room at Thionville

Centre right
*A heavy steel door closes a rifle embrasure guarding a searchlight
position at Thionville*

Right
*An underground passage joining two gun battery positions: electric
cables run along the wall and the trunking of the air conditioning
plant can be seen suspended from the ceiling*

shallow, filled with barbed wire entanglements. Lying within the wire armoured observation posts and machine-gun emplacements communicated back to the main forts through a long deep tunnel. From the air practically nothing showed, for the forts were dug deep into the ground and encased within thick concrete. Each fort had its own concrete barracks built deep underground and independent, although joined by tunnels to its neighbours. The electricity supply was central, powered by nine diesel engines, but in all other respects the batteries could function independently. Each had a hand-operated system which controlled the ventilation and moved the armoured turrets. Each had separate 48 volt armoured searchlight positions to illuminate the approaches flanked by concealed rifle positions. Everything could be worked from inside. Even the gun barrels could be changed and the cartridges re-calibred so that they could be re-used. The telephone system was duplicated with speaking tubes running from the command post to the gun positions and the observation posts.

The merit of the feste solution lay in the fact that it could contain all the elements required for defence within a loosely grouped and irregular layout. The heavy weapons were sufficiently deployed and independently worked to prevent their being obliterated by a concentrated enemy bombardment, and flanking weapons were sufficiently closely assembled to allow adequate mutual defence. Finally close defence, in the form of entrenched infantry, was supported by the other two weapons.

A NEW CENTURY:
OLD CONCEPTS

Although there were occasions in the First World War when permanent fortifications such as Tsingtao and Przemysl put up a stout resistance, the final establishment of a long period of stalemate was due to the exploitation of field fortifications stiffened by wire entanglements and criss-crossed by the rapid fire of machine-guns.

Tsingtao Fortress was the pride of the German colonies in the Far East. The port lay on a peninsula of the China coast and in front stood four armoured forts constructed at great expense with cupola batteries of 70 centimetre howitzers and 60 and 38 centimetre guns. Beyond these stretched the minefield and the wire entanglements, illuminated by searchlights in disappearing cupolas, and beyond all that infantry trenches. The Japanese attacked on 27 August 1914 but it took them a month to reduce the German positions during which time the Germans carried out, for the first time, an aerial bombardment on the Japanese ships that were shelling the forts.

Przemysl was the Austrian Verdun, fortified by a ring of 19 large forts and 23 smaller works designed after the manner of Brialmont and stretching in a circuit of 48 kilometres. The forts, originally constructed in stone in the 1880s, were later modified by the addition of heavy concrete as those at Ver-

dun had been treated. The Russian siege opened on 11 November 1914 but the fortress stood firm for over four months until all food was exhausted.

The value of field fortifications had been known from earlier times. They had been used with effect in the Italian wars at the turn of the fifteenth century, but the long period which had seen the growth of the most elaborate systems of permanent fortification had tended to cloud any assessment of the value of their more temporary relative. The Russo-Turkish War of 1877 redressed the balance and brought to the attention of the western army commands the value of hastily improvised earth defences which received the name 'provisional fortification'. In about six weeks around Adrianople the Turks threw up a chain of 24 provisional redoubts, and farther back, barring the road to Constantinople, Bluhm Pasha, with equal rapidity, constructed the famous Lines of Tschataldscha. General Montgomery has summed up the contribution: 'The success of the resistance put up by the Turks astonished contemporary Europe. Osman Pasha's field fortifications pointed to the character of future fighting between armies armed with rifles'.

The Russo-Japanese War of 1904 only acted to strengthen the conviction that the immediate future lay with field

A Russian field fort one mile south of
Liao-Yang, 1904

fortifications. The military textbooks had to be largely re-written. The forts south of Liao-Yang were well-prepared earthworks surrounded by wet ditches and meshed with wire entanglements, and beyond lay two rings of deep circular pits each with a sharp spike upon which to trap a fallen man, and the inner ring was criss-crossed with barbed wire. Machine-guns covered the obstacles from the angles of the fort and the garrison had well-protected bombproof living accommodation. Eleven similar redoubts guarded the town and the Japanese paid dearly for their capture. One redoubt alone took a death toll of 3,000.

The main defences of Port Arthur stretched in a zone five kilometres deep. Locked in a web of permanent forts was a tangled mass of hastily thrown-up redoubts and excavated trenches which kept the Japanese at bay for six months. The Japanese infantry were held up on barbed wire, mown down by machine-gun and rifle fire and illuminated by star shells and searchlights when they sought the concealment of darkness. Only after recourse to extensive sapping and mining could General Nogi's men slowly break through to the town with heavy loss of life: 60,000 were killed and over 33,000 wounded. Both the price they paid and the effort they expended in finally overcoming the defence forecast the holocaust of the Western Front.

Curiously, nations reacted differently to the conditions brought about by the long periods of stalemate experienced in the First World War and to the heavy losses incurred in capturing each yard of ground. Whereas France sought to take advantage of what appeared to be a situation biased in favour of defence, Germany searched for a method to break through or circumvent any lines of defence in a future lightning war which would paralyse her enemies. Benefiting from the development of two weapons, the fast tank and the dive-bomber, she prepared to implement a modified Schlieffen Plan which had failed in 1914 largely through lack of speed on the part of the attackers. Germany had not been able to advance on two sides of a triangle as fast as France could move her armies into position across the shorter base of the triangle by means of an efficient railroad system.

The French answer to the threat of invasion was the construction of the Maginot Line, the most ambitious and the most thorough piece of permanent fortification the world had ever seen. It was to be misjudged by public opinion and used as a scapegoat for the rapid defeat of France in the Second World War.

The defence of the frontier had occupied French military minds for generations. Louis XIV, using Vauban, had built a large number of individual fortresses at enormous cost. In 1874 General Séré de Rivières proposed the construction of a barrier to run all the way from Calais to Nice with, behind it, a general defensive scheme stretching in depth as far as Paris. The idea was to cover the whole line of frontier, to absorb the initial shock of attack and provide time for the full mobilisation of the French army. This defensive thinking was deep-rooted in France. The line of 1874 was to follow the most easily defensible ground, the heights of Meuse and the Moselle, rather than to attempt to defend the artificially created frontier of the country.

The purpose of the Maginot Line was quite different. It was designed to form a shield for Alsace and Lorraine, and to protect the vital iron and steel industry of the Saar. And it was not intended to form a continuous line for the defence of the whole of France.

The line got its name from André Maginot who as Minister of War was the driving force who got the project accepted. The basic design was worked out in 1927 by General Belhague, Inspector General of Fortifications, with the help of Frossard. Its design can be seen as a culmination of the long process of development which had evolved by way of the strongly protected underground fort with guns firing from heavily armoured cupolas. The French were fully conversant with the German feste at Metz.

Because the works are underground and somewhat confined the line is hardly photogenic. Its functioning can best be understood from a description. There were three elements in the scheme. First the *maison-fortes*, which were small reinforced barracks placed close to the frontier and at any vulnerable points likely to be the object of any spearheaded attack. Their purpose was to sound the alarm and they were to be occupied by mobile forces. Then about three kilometres to the rear began *avant-postes*, detached outposts constructed of heavy reinforced concrete in which a garrison was to be permanently on duty manning the 47- or 65-millimetre guns. These outposts covered all the likely approaches to the main fortresses of the line and were supported by anti-tank and anti-infantry barriers like traps, railway lines embedded in the ground, concrete pyramids and barbed wire entanglements, all covered by machine-guns and anti-tank guns. Behind these came the main fortification which varied according to the nature of the terrain and the task it was likely to face. Principally it consisted of a series of detached heavy reinforced concrete casemates with large powerful fortresses

placed five to eight kilometres apart. The casemates were dug into hillsides or sometimes enveloped in an artificial mound and consisted of two levels of accommodation, the troops sleeping and storing ammunition on the lower level and firing their anti-tank guns through small embrasures on the upper level. The front was protected by a three metre ditch and from the roof projected small cupolas housing mortars or quick-firing guns, and periscopes through which the defenders could survey the surrounding countryside. Each casemate had its own lighting and ventilating system. Sometimes two were joined to form neighbours, connected by underground passages and capable of giving each other supporting fire.

The forts are the best known and most elaborate elements of the defence. They varied in size and some were capable of holding 1,200 men. Like a small town cut into the ground their accommodation descended in storey under storey into the depth of the earth. Only the small armoured cupolas of the retractable turrets which carried the artillery of the fort showed above ground. Armament ranged from anti-tank weapons to heavy 81- and 135-millimetre guns. Adjoining each turret was an expense magazine and quarters for the troops on duty at the gun. Liftshafts and staircases penetrated into the ground to the plotting room which was linked to observation turrets and gun positions, then down through the operations room to the four or five storeys of barrack accommodation. Down again to the power plant which gave the fort its life, electric light, power and pressure ventilation to exclude fumes and poison gas. Deep down lay the kitchens, the storage space, the main magazines and the hospital. Horizontal passages connected the main quarters to the outlying armoured gun positions and the two main entrances, the passages capable of being closed at intervals by heavy armourplated doors. In the bowels of the earth, some 23–30 metres down lay the telephone operations room and intelligence nerve centre of the defence. The 'metro' ran at this level, capable of moving troops on small electric trains at speed and in safety.

The French had learnt their lesson at Verdun and now the forts were deep and encased in such heavy concrete as to be capable of withstanding the heaviest bombardment. Without fear of damage each could call upon its neighbour for covering fire so that any parachutists or assault troops who might penetrate to the cupolas of a fort would be killed off by the guns of the forts adjoining it. In Belgium, Fort Eben Emael fell in 1940 because the Germans used dive-bombers

to crater the ground in front of the fort and then landed parachutists and glider troops who were able to run from crater to crater until eventually they could, with impunity, place charges on the very barrels of the guns of the fort. This fort was not capable of receiving supporting fire from neighbours. The forts and outposts of the Maginot Line were only part of the French defensive scheme for they were meant to be supplemented by the guns and armour of the field army encamped in the intervals.

However the line did not rest with the defence of Alsace and Lorraine. The population of France was falling and it was realised that the shortage of manpower in the important age groups would become apparent after 1935 and would be most serious by 1939. Any system which would conserve manpower would help France. It was therefore decided to extend the Maginot Line to Longwy near the Forest of Ardennes on the west and to Basel on the Swiss frontier. The extensions, although formidable, were not built in the same massive manner as the original part of the line. North from Longwy lay the long gap to the Channel ports, to be defended by older fortresses and the main French field armies. Many Frenchmen agreed with Pétain that 'the northern frontier can only be defended by advancing into Belgium'. For political reasons such a step could not be taken by the French without the wholehearted collaboration of the Belgians, who were reluctant to compromise their neutrality for fear of offending Germany. In the event their attitude gave them no protection against Germany and no co-ordinated assistance from the allies. In a *blitzkrieg* attack the German armies in 1940 flooded through Belgium into France, splitting the French army and isolating the British in the great right hook which had been the essence of the Schlieffen Plan of 1906. Its success exceeded all expectations, even those of the German General Staff. From the Maginot Line the French moved out their remaining field armies and thinned down the garrison. But left half naked, the defences still proved their capabilities. In a series of frontal attacks the German army was able to make no progress except on the little fort of La Ferté which, lying on the extreme left of the line and being partly unsupported, fell to the Germans on 19 May 1940. No other fort on the Maginot Line fell to German attack and none was seriously damaged. Only after the downfall of France and on instructions from the French government did the Maginot Line surrender. It had achieved its purpose, to defend Alsace-Lorraine and to force the Germans to concentrate their attack at the one point where the French field armies should have been ready and able to hold them. If the French nation was lulled into a feeling of false security, it was due largely to the misleading articles in the press which falsely suggested that the whole line of the French frontier was invulnerable. The main cause of the collapse of France must be sought in the thoroughness of the German preparations and the brilliance and audacity of their attack.

Other nations had been convinced of the validity of the Maginot Line and had sought to copy it. The Czechs had modelled their defences on it so that when the Germans marched into the country they were able to study its construction at leisure. In Holland and Belgium there were less powerful versions in the Grebbe, Peel and Dyle Lines.

The Germans in 1936 began construction on their great West Wall. It is sometimes called the Siegfried Line, which is confusing, because that was also the name given to a defensive line built by the Germans in 1918 from Cambrai to St Quentin. By 1940 the West Wall stretched from the Swiss frontier to Aachen in the north. It was called by the British troops in France the Siegfried Line upon which they were determined to 'hang out our washing'. The line was hurried in execution and its forts were less complex than those in the Maginot Line, but it was an immensely wide fortified area stretching in places to a depth of 32 kilometres. It consisted of a series of heavy reinforced concrete bunkers similar in conception to the French *avant-postes*, whose fire criss-crossed the area and supported the main forts which acted as the strongpoints of the defence. The purpose of the West Wall was to hold a front with the minimum number of troops against any possible French counterattack, whilst allowing the main armies to attack Russia or the gap in the defences on the left of the French lines.

These mighty fortifications provide a fitting climax to any study of military architecture. Whether they will be the last of the line of development stretching back to ancient Mesopotamia, or the beginning of a new underground world, predicted by H. G. Wells and occasioned by the devastating power of atomic explosion, only time can tell. Man has shown an infinite capacity to protect himself by artificial means: let us hope that this facility does not now desert him.

GLOSSARY

ADVANCED WORKS those placed beyond the glacis but near enough to receive protection from the main defences.

APPROACHES trenches dug by besiegers and running from their parallel trenches in a zigzag pattern so as not to be exposed to enfilade fire.

BAILEY courtyard attached to a fortified mound or motte.

BALLISTA large early weapon used to hurl stones.

BANQUETTE footstand for infantry behind a parapet.

BARBETTE raised platform from which guns can fire over a parapet.

BARBICAN advanced work protecting the gate of a town or a castle or the approaches to a bridge.

BARRIER-FORTS detached forts built to hold up an enemy advance at vulnerable positions like mountain passes; alternatively barrier forts are mutually supporting works which form a line of defence as opposed to an enceinte of a town.

BARTIZAN battlemented turret projecting from the top of a tower or wall.

BASCULE counterbalanced drawbridge.

BASTION here used to describe a work which projects from the main walls of a fortress or fortified town and is shaped in the form of an irregular pentagon as developed by Italian engineers at the end of the fifteenth and the beginning of the sixteenth centuries.

BASTIONETTES small bastions attached to the salient angles of bastions in order to increase the intensity of flanking fire which can be brought to bear along their faces.

BATARDEAU knife-edged barrier built across the ditch to dam its waters but designed so that enemy troops would have difficulty in crossing it.

BATTER (of a wall) its inward inclination from the base.

BERM ridge below a parapet to prevent earth falling into a moat.

BOMBPROOF building or a part of the defences constructed to withstand cannon balls or shells.

BONNET small triangular work in front of the salient angle of a bastion or a ravelin to give it additional protection from enfilade fire.

BREACH gap blown in fortifications by cannon or mine.

BRISURE break in the line of a curtain wall in order to expand the space for guns in the flank of a bastion.

Below
Plan of the citadel at Antwerp illustrating terms used in the glossary; from seventh edition of Encyclopaedia Britannica

A   Curtain
B   Bastion
C   Covered way
D   Ditch
E   Ravelin
F   Casemates
G   Caponier

Right
Plans of traces to illustrate terms in the glossary; from the seventh edition of Encyclopaedia Britannica

J	Place of arms	Q	Traverses	Y	Embrasures
K	Covered way	R	Flank of bastion	Z	Parapet
L	Salient place of arms	S	Curtain	AA	Glacis
M	Ditch	T	Tenaille	BB	Foot of glacis
N	Shoulder	U	Gorge of ravelin	CC	Ridge of Glacis
O	Bastion	W	Gorge of bastion	DD	Furrow of glacis
P	Face of bastion	X	Ravelin	HB	Line of defence

VAUBAN'S FIRST SYSTEM.

$A\,B = 360\ \text{Yards}.$

$C\,D = \dfrac{360}{6}$

$A\,E = \dfrac{2}{7}\ \text{of}\ A\,B$

10 20 40 60   120   180   240   300   360 *Yards*

OUTWORKS

a-Detached Lunette. b-Fleche, c-Lunettes, d-Bonnet, e-Entrenched Bastions, f-Batardeau, g-Hornwork, h-Caponier, k-Tenaillon

30 60   120   180   240   300   360 *Yards*

*Section through a fortification by Wilhelm
Dilich to illustrate terms*

CALIBRE size of the bore of a gun.

CAPANNATO triangular bombproof room pointing towards the direction of attack, its faces pierced by loopholes for defenders' guns.

CAPONIER sheltered passage across the ditch leading to outworks and sometimes providing additional flanking fire for the ditch.

CASEMATES vaulted chambers in the ramparts used as barracks or gun positions.

CAVALIER a high work, built on a bastion or a curtain, once described as 'standing up like a cavalryman'.

CHEMIN DE RONDE a passage on top of the scarp wall, protected by a small parapet from which musketeers could observe the glacis at close range and prevent the placing of scaling ladders. It was generally abandoned at the time of Vauban because it was exposed to artillery fire and could easily be destroyed.

CIRCUMVALLATION the entrenchment cut by besiegers around any place being invested.

CITADEL main fortress of a town, put there to dominate or protect the town.

COMMAND any work raised higher than another is said to command it.

CORDON projecting top course of the scarp wall.

COUNTERFORTS buttresses built behind scarp walls in order to strengthen them.

COUNTERGUARDS more extensive outworks than bonnets; they are usually triangular, open at the back and cover the faces of bastions, ravelins and redans.

COUNTERSCARP outer wall of the ditch.

COUPURE a cut in the parapet of a bastion or a ravelin.

COVERED WAY broad space on the top of the counterscarp protected by a parapet from enemy fire.

CREMAILLERE indented or zigzag trace usually provided to give additional positions for defending guns.

CRENELLE an embrasure; the gap in a parapet through which archers or gunners can fire; hence crenellate.

CROCHETS passages made round the head of every traverse to allow troops to bypass the traverse when moving along the covered way.

CROWNWORK powerful exposed work consisting of a central bastion supported by two half or demi-bastions.

CUNETTE small moat to drain water out of a ditch into a well.

CUPOLA armoured dome designed to house guns, searchlights or observation equipment for an underground fort.

CURTAIN main wall of a defensive work; it is reinforced by bastions or towers placed at a distance from the main defences, defending the approaches without supporting fire from the main fortification.

DEMI-LUNE an outwork resembling a bastion with a crescent-shaped gorge.

DITCH excavated line forming an obstacle; it may be wet or dry.

DONJON French word for a keep; should not be confused with dungeon or prison.

DRUM-TOWER a massive cylindrical tower.

ECHAUGETTE a stone sentry box cantilevered from the angle of a bastion.

EMBRASURE opening cut in a parapet, in early work usually wider at the rear than at the front, through which a gun can be fired.

ENCEINTE area enclosed within the main line of ramparts, but excluding any outworks.

ENTRENCHED CAMPS provide safe refuge for an army to assemble or regroup behind permanent fortifications; entrenched camps may be towns or cities.

ESCALADE the climbing of walls with the help of ladders.

ESPLANADE open space behind the walls of a town or between the citadel and the houses of a town: *see* pomerio.

EXPENSE MAGAZINE powder store containing enough made-up ammunition to last 24 hours.

FACE (of a bastion) the exposed outer wall between the salient point and the flank.

FAUSSE-BRAYE an outer enceinte, separated from and lower than the curtain wall, in front of which it normally stands. Used by sixteenth century and seventeenth century engineers, it was soon abandoned as, under bombardment, splinters from the wall behind wounded its defenders and it came to be called a 'shot trap'.

FESTE name given to a group of defences which includes long-range and close-support artillery and infantry.

FIRE, in plan, is either direct when it comes from the front; oblique, slanting when it strikes at a very small angle; enfilade when it comes in from the side, or reverse when it strikes the rear of a defended work.

FLANK part of a defensive work designed to provide flanking fire in order to defend another work; it is the part of a bastion between the face and the curtain wall; to flank is to protect a work with flanking fire; that is, fire from a flank.

FLECHE arrow-shaped work, smaller than a redan or a lunette, placed at the foot of a glacis.

FORT (as distinct from a castle) building designed primarily for defence; living accommodation is only incidental.

FORTRESS name given to a major fortified work or fortified city; examples of first-class fortresses are Strasbourg, Antwerp and Paris.

FOUGASSE hole dug in the rock facing the enemy, filled with a barrel of gunpowder and wood and then piled with rocks so that it can be fired like a mortar.

FRONT OF FORTIFICATION distance between the salient points of two adjoining bastions.

GABION cylindrical wicker basket filled with earth and used for field fortification.

GALLERY OF THE COUNTERSCARP bombproof defensive position on the outside of the ditch, designed to defend that ditch.

GLACIS long gentle slope beyond the ditch which is kept clear of all obstacles; it starts at the crest of the parapet of the covered way and its foot stretches out into the countryside.

GORGE the neck, or the interior side, of a bastion or an outwork.

GRAZING FIRE skims over a surface.

HORNWORK an important outwork consisting of a curtain wall flanked by two demi-bastions.

KEEP the strongest and last defensible tower of a castle; *see* donjon and mastio.

LINE OF DEFENCE is drawn from a curtain wall or the flank of a bastion across the face of the adjoining bastion.

LUNETTE large advanced work shaped like a detached bastion.

MACHICOLATION projecting gallery of timber, brick or stone from which combustibles can be dropped on soldiers attacking the foot of a wall.

MAGISTRAL LINE crest of the scarp of a fortification; in drawings it is always drawn thicker than other lines.

MANGONEL machine for throwing stones.

MANTLET movable protective screen used in attacking a place.

MASTIO Italian term for a keep or donjon.

MERLON solid part of a parapet, between two crenelles or embrasures.

MOTTE steep artificial mound of earth, forming the base of many eleventh and twelfth century castles.

ONAGER ancient stone-throwing machine constructed with a single arm.

ORILLION ear attached to the angle between the face and the flank of a bastion.

PARALLEL ditch dug by besiegers parallel to the works they intend to attack; from it, zigzag approaches are made to the next, more advanced, parallel.

PARAPET breastwork on top of ramparts, thick enough to cover troops behind it.

PERPENDICULAR FORTIFICATION system devised by Montalembert in 1776

consisting of a series of tenailles rather like the teeth of a saw.

PIAZZA BASSA a casemate in a flank for artillery to cover the ditch and enfilade the curtain.

PLACE-OF-ARMS space for troops to assemble; salient if it is at the outer point of a covered way, and re-entrant if it is at the inner point.

PLUNGING FIRE poured directly on to an enemy from a higher position.

POINT BLANK FIRE the axis of the gun is aimed directly at the object being attacked.

POLYGONAL FORTIFICATION devised by Montalembert and consisted of faces, forming salient angles only or re-entering angles of small depth, flanked by a powerful caponier constructed in the main ditch.

POMERIO open space between the walls of a fortress or town and the outermost houses; *see* esplanade.

PORTCULLIS grilles shod with iron and lowered between the towers of a gatehouse to form a barrier in front of the door.

POSTERN sallyport, a small tunnel leading out of the fortifications.

RAMPART fortified embankment topped by a parapet.

RAVELIN triangular outwork, with or without flanks, usually placed in the ditch in front of a curtain.

REDAN triangular work in advance of a main fortification, similar to but slightly larger than a fleche; a redan system of fortification consists of a series of triangular works in the form of a serrated edge.

REDOUBT small work in a bastion or ravelin, or one placed beyond the glacis but within range of muskets on the covered way.

REDUIT keep; a last stronghold for the garrison to prolong the defence.

RETIRADE device for breaking the face of a long bastion to allow sufficient space for a few men to fire on an enemy attempting to venture into the re-entering angle of the ditch.

RETRENCHMENT (or retirata) work constructed behind a bastion in order to strengthen it; interior retrenchments are designed to give a garrison the means of vigorously defending the breaches without exposing the place to be carried by storm.

REVETMENT retaining wall in a ditch, built to face earthen ramparts.

RING-FORTS built at the end of the nineteenth century to form an outer ring of detached works covering a fortress or an entrenched camp.

ROCCA Italian word for a fort as distinct from a castle which in addition to being a stronghold is usually the abode of a wealthy or aristocratic family.

SALIENT ANGLE outward point of a bastion or other projecting work.

SALLYPORT *see* postern.

SAP zigzag trench cut by besiegers towards a besieged fortress; *see* approaches.

SCARP interior wall of a ditch.

SHOULDER OF THE BASTION angle between its face and its flank; the orillion sometimes supports the shoulder.

SPIKING driving a nail into the touch-hole of a large gun in order to disable it.

SPUR usually an arrow-shaped outwork projecting from the face of a curtain wall.

STORMPROOF WORK defended position from which the enemy can be destroyed as fast as they approach.

TALUS sloping wall, thicker at its base; *see* batter.

TENAILLE small low-lying work, placed between adjoining bastions to provide additional cover for the curtain wall.

TENAILLE TRACE succession of redans joined at right angles to form a front of defence which resembles the teeth of a saw.

TENAILLON irregularly shaped outwork placed to cover the face of a ravelin.

TERREPLEIN originally the gently sloping ground behind a parapet; later became the natural ground surface of a fortified work from which guns and troops operated, protected by an artificial parapet.

TORTOISE small mobile siege tower containing a ram.

TOURS-MODELES French coastal towers constructed by Napoleon.

TRACE ground plan of a fortification.

TRADITORE BATTERIES provide fire to the flanks and rear only.

TRAVERSES barriers constructed on places like the covered way to protect troops and guns from enemy flanking fire.

TWYDALL PROFILE gentle slope from the crest of a fortification to about 15 or 20 feet below natural ground level; at its foot an unclimbable steel palisade and barbed wire entanglements were placed; it was sometimes used at the end of the nineteenth century in place of a deep ditch.

WINGS long sides of exposed fortifications such as hornworks and crownworks.

BIBLIOGRAPHY

Source material arranged in the order in which the authors appear in the text.

VITRUVIUS,
de architectura,
Rome 1486

VEGETIUS RENATUS, FLAVIUS,
de re militari,
Rome 1494

PIZZANO, CRISTINA DA,
The Book of Fayttes of Armes and of Chivualrye, etc,
Westminster 1489

TACCOLA, MARIANUS JACOBUS, called,
De machinis libri X,
ms. Paris, Bibl. Nat, lat. 7239

KYESER, KONRAD,
Bellifortis,
c 1405,
ms. Göttingen, University Library, cod. phil. 63

GUIDO DA VIGEVANO,
Thesaurus Regis Franciae,
ms. Paris, Bibl. Nat.

TARTAGLIA, NICCOLO,
Sul modo di fortificare le città rispetto la forma,
Venice 1536
Nova scientia,
Venice 1537
Quesiti et inventioni diverse de N. Tartalea Brisciano,
Venice 1546
Three Books of Colloquies concerning the Arte of shooting in great and small pieces of Artillerie . . .,
London 1588

ALBERTI, LEON BATTISTA,
De re aedificatoria,
Rome 1485

MACHIAVELLI, NICCOLO,
Libro dell'arte della guerra,
Florence 1521

FILARETE, ANTONIO FRANCESCO AVERLINO, called,
ms. Florence, Bibl. Naz, II. I. 40

FRANCESCO DI GIORGIO MARTINI,
Trattato dell' architettura civile e militare,
Siena, Bibl. Comunale, S IV 4

PHILIP, Duke of Cleves,
Instruction de toutes manieres de guerroyer,
Paris 1558

LEONARDO DA VINCI,
ms.
Paris, Bibl. Institut, ms. A–M
Milan, Bibl. Ambros, Cod. Atlanticus

DÜRER, ALBRECHT,
Etliche underricht zu befestigung der stett, schloss und flecken,
Nuremberg 1527

VALLE, BATTISTA DELLA,
Vallo: libro continente appertentie ad Capitanii,

retenere & fortificare una Citta cō bastioni, con novi artificii de fusco aggiōti . . . et de expugnare una Citta, etc,
Venice 1524

ALBERTI, LEON BATTISTA,
I primi tre libri della famiglia,
(c 1435–44)
See Mancini, G., *I libri della famiglia,*
Florence 1908

IVE, PAUL,
The practice of fortification . . .,
London 1589

CATANEO, PIETRO,
I quattro primi libri di architettura di P. Cataneo,
Venice 1554

SCRIVÀ, PEDRO LUIS,
Apologia en excusacion y favor de las fabricas del reino de Napoles, 1538,
ms. Bibl. Roy, Madrid

LANTERI, GIACOMO,
Due dialoghi . . . del modo di disegnare le piante delle fortezze, ecc,
Venice 1557
Delle offese et difese delle città et fortezza di G. Lanteri . . . con due discorsi d'architettura militare d'A. Lupicini,
5 pt, Venice 1601

MAGGI, GIROLAMO,
Della fortificatione delle città, di G. Maggi e del Capitan I. Castriotto . . . Libri III,
Venice 1564

CATANEO, GIROLAMO,
Opera nuoua di fortificare, offendere et difendere . . .,
Brescia 1564

MARCHI, FRANCESCO DE, Capitano,
Della architettura militare . . . libri tre,
Brescia 1599

LAPARELLI, FRANCESCO,
Codex (c 1566),
ms. Cortona, Laparelli-Pitti coll.

ALGHISI, GALASSO,
Delle fortificationi . . . libri tre,
Venice 1570

SCAMOZZI, VINCENZO,
L'idea dell' architettura universale, ecc,
2 pt, Venice 1615

SPECKLE, DANIELE,
Architectura von Vestungen,
Strasbourg 1589

DE LA TREILLE, VEROIL
Manière de Fortifier les villes et châteaux,
Paris 1557

ERRARD DE BAR-LE-DUC, JEAN,
La fortification reduicte en art et demonstrée . . .,
Frankfurt-on-Main 1604

BRAUN, GEORGIUS, and HOGENBERG, FRANZ,
Civitates orbis terrarum,
Cologne 1572

MERIAN, MATTHÄUS, the elder,
Topographia, etc,
Amsterdam 1644

FER, NICOLAS DE,
Les Forces de L'Europe ou Description des principales villes avec leur Fortifications, etc,
8 pt in 2 vol, Paris 1690–95

STURM, LEONHARD CHRISTOPH,
Le veritable Vauban, se montrant au lieu du faux Vauban qui a couru jusqu'ici par le monde . . .,
The Hague 1710
Leonhard Christoph Sturms Architectura militaris hypothetico-edectica . . .,
Nürnberg 1736

FLORIANI, PIETRO PAOLO,
Difesa et offesa delle piazze,
Macerata 1630

VAUBAN, SEBASTIEN LE PRESTRE DE,
Traité . . . de l'attaque des places . . . publiée . . . par M. Augoyat (Traité de la défense des places . . . publiée . . . par M. le Baron de Valazé),
2 pt, Paris 1829
De l'attaque et de la défense des places,
2 vol, The Hague 1737–42

CORMONTAINGNE, LOUIS DE,
L'Architecture militaire, ou l'Art de fortifier,
3 pt, The Hague 1741

FREITAG, ADAM,
Architectura militaris nova et aucta, oder Newe vermehrte Fortification, von Regular Vestungen, von Irregular Vestungen und Aussen wercken, etc,
Leyden 1631

COEHORN, MENNO VAN, Baron,
Nieuwe Vestingbouw . . . van de Fransche royale seshoek . . .,
Leeuwarden 1702
The New Method of Fortification, translated from the original Dutch . . . by Tho. Savery,
London 1705

MONTALEMBERT, MARC RENÉ, Marquis de,
La Fortification Perpendiculaire; ou, essai sur plusieurs manières de fortifier,
Paris 1776–84

LANDSBERG, JOHANN HEINRICH VON,
Nouveaux plans et projets de fortification, pour défendre et attaquer les places,
The Hague 1731

CARNOT, LAZARE-NICOLAS MARGUERITE, Count,
De la défense des places fortes . . . Mémoire sur la fortification primitive, etc,
Paris 1810

PASLEY, CHARLES WILLIAM, Sir
A Course of Elementary Fortification . . .
second edition,
2 vol. London & Chatham 1822

YULE, HENRY, Sir,
Fortification for Officers of the Army and Students of Military History, with illustrations and notes,
Edinburgh and London 1851

FERGUSSON, JAMES,
An Essay on a Proposed New System of Fortification; with hints for its application to our national defences,
London 1849

LENDY, AUGUSTE FRÉDÉRIC,
Elements of Fortification, field and permanent,
London 1857
Treatise on Fortification; or Lectures delivered to Officers reading for the Staff,
London 1862

CLAUSEWITZ, KARL PHILIPP GOTLIEB VON,
Vom Kriege,
Berlin 1832–34

Other general works used in the preparation of this volume

ACKERMAN, JAMES,
The Architecture of Michelangelo,
2 vols, London 1961

ALBARIC, ALAIN,
Aigues-Mortes,
Château-de-Valence (Gard) 1968

ALBERTI, LEON BATTISTA,
Ten Books on Architecture,
transl. into Italian by Cosimo Bartoli, into English by James Leoni, edited by Joseph Rykwert, facsimile, London 1965

ANDERSON, WILLIAM,
Castles of Europe from Charlemagne to the Renaissance,
London 1970

ANON,
Sketch of the Defences of the Western and Swiss Frontiers of Germany,
London 1888

ANON,
Nouveau Manuel de Fortification Permanente,
Paris 1895

ASHMEAD-BARTLETT, ELLIS,
Port Arthur: the Siege and Capitulation,
London 1906

BAINBRIDGE, Lt-Col,
Notes on the Defence of Coasts,
in 'Professional Papers of the Royal Engineers',
new series, Vol. IX, 1860

BALFOUR, ALAN,
Portsmouth,
London 1970

BARNETT, CORRELLI,
Britain and her Army: 1509–1970,
London 1970

BASCAPE, G. C., & PEROGALLI, C.,
Castelli del Lazio,
Milan 1968

BELFIELD, EVERSLEY,
Sieges,
London 1967

BERTI, LUCIANO,
Studies for the fortifications of Florence (1528–30) in *The Complete Works of Michelangelo,* Vol. II,
London 1966

BISSET, CHARLES,
The Theory and Construction of Fortification,
London 1751

LE BLOND, M.,
The Military Engineer or a treatise on the attack and defence of all kinds of fortified places,
London 1759

BOASE, T. S. R.,
Castles and Churches of the Crusading Kingdom,
London 1967

BOINET, A.,
Le Château de Pierrefonds,
Paris 1930

BORDWINE, JOSEPH,
Memoir of a proposed new system of permanent fortification,
London 1834

BORGATTI, MARIANO,
La fortificazione permanente contemporanea,
2 vols, Turin 1898

BOUDET, JACQUES,
The Ancient Art of Warfare,
2 vols, London 1966

BRAUN & HOGENBERG,
Civitates orbis terrarum: 1572–1618,
facsimile in 6 parts, III volumes; introduction by R. A. Skelton,
Amsterdam 1965

BRIALMONT, HENRI,
La Défense des Côtes, etc,
Brussels 1896

BROCKMAN, ERIC,
The Two Sieges of Rhodes, 1480–1522,
London 1969

BRUIJN, C. A. DE, & REINDERS, H. R.,
Nederlandse Vestingen,
Bussum 1967

BURGOYNE, JOHN F., General Sir,
Coast Batteries,
'Corps Papers of the Royal Engineers',
1st vol., 1849–50, paper XV
On Coast Defences,
in 'Professional Papers of the Royal Engineers',
new series, vol. VI, 1857

BUTTIN, FRANÇOIS,
Les Propulseurs de Léonard de Vinci,
Paris 1965,
'Bull. de la S.P.F.' LXI, No. 1,
1964

CALVI, IGNAZIO,
L'Architettura Militare di Leonardo da Vinci,
Milan 1943
'Military Engineering and Arms' in

Leonardo da Vinci,
London 1957

CARNOT, L-N. M.,
*A Treatise on the defence of Fortified Places:
Written under the direction and published by
command of Buonaparte*,
transl. Baron de Montalembert,
London 1814

CASSELL, R. J.,
Cassell's History of the Russo-Japanese War,
3 vols, London, Paris, New York &
Melbourne 1904–05

CEOLA, MARIO,
La guerra sotterranea attraverso i secoli,
Rovereto 1939

CLARKE, GEORGE SYDENHAM, Sir,
Miscellaneous Papers, 1884–88,
Chatham 1888
*Fortification: its past achievements, recent
developments and future progress*,
2nd ed., London 1907

CLARKE, G. S., & O'CALLAGHAN, P.,
*Report on 100-ton Guns at Gibraltar and
Malta*,
War Office 1887

CLAUSEWITZ, KARL VON,
On War,
transl. O. J. Matthijs Jolles,
New York 1943

CLAVIJO, DON SALVADOR,
*Extracts from an analysis and comparison of the
French and German Systems of Fortification*,
published in the 'Spanish Royal Engineers'
Annual Papers',
transl. Capt. Hutchinson, RE, in
'Professional Papers of the Royal
Engineers',
new series, Vol. VIII, 1859

COCKLE, MAURICE J. D.,
A Bibliography of Military Books up to 1642,
London 1957

COEHORN, MENNON, Baron de,
*Nouvelle Fortification tant pour un terrain bas
& humide que sec & élévé.
Représentée en trois manières, sur le contenu
intérieur de l'hexagone à la françoise*,
The Hague 1741

CORMONTAINGNE,
*Memorial de Cormontaingne pour l'attaque des
places, etc*,
posthumous work, with notes by
de Bousmard,
Berlin 1803

CORNEY, ARTHUR,
Fortifications in Old Portsmouth – a guide,
Portsmouth 1968
Southsea Castle,
Portsmouth 1968

CORPS ROYAL DU GÉNIE,
Memoires sur la Fortification Perpendiculaire,
Paris 1786

CRAMWINCKEL, J. C.,
*Duurzame Versterkingskunst, Leerboek voor de
cadetten van alle wapens, Tweede deel*,
Militaire Academie Amsterdam 1918

CROCKER, J.,
History of the Fortifications of Malta,
General Staff, Malta Command,
Malta 1920

DAVIES, WILLIAM,
Fort Regent,
Jersey, C.I. 1971

DILICH, JOHANN WILHELM,
Peribologia,
Frankfurt-on-Main 1640

EGYPT,
*Report on the defences of Alexandria and on the
results of the action of 11 July 1882*,
War Office, London 1883

EIS, EGON,
The Forts of Folly – the history of an illusion,
transl. A. J. Pomerans,
London 1959

FALLS, CYRIL, editor,
Great Military Battles,
London 1964

FEDDEN, ROBIN, & THOMSON, JOHN,
Crusader Castles,
London 1957

FRANCESCO DI GIORGIO MARTINI
*Trattati di architettura, ingegneria e arte
militare*,
ed. Corrado Maltese,
Milan, nd

FRASER, T., Captain,
The Attack of Fortresses in the Future,
Royal Engineer Prize Essay 1876,
London 1877

GILLE, BERTRAND,
The Renaissance Engineers,
London 1966

GIOVANNI, GUSTAVO,
Antonio da Sangallo il Giovane,
2 vols, Rome 1959

GIROUARD, MARK,
Castles on the Ghana Coast
in 'Country Life' 1961, 9 Nov.,
pp. 1122–5

GREY, F. W., Admiral Sir,
President of Committee,
*Report of the Committee appointed to enquire
into the construction, condition and cost of the
fortifications erected, or in course of erection,
under 30th and 31st Vict. and previous
Statutes*,
presented to both Houses of Parliament,
London 1869

GUGLIELMOTTI, A.,
*Storia della fortificazione nella spiaggia
romana*,
(Vol. V. della Storia della Marina
Pontificia),
Rome 1887

GUIDO, MARGARET,
Syracuse,
Syracuse 1958

HAGUE, DOUGLAS B.,
Penrhyn Castle,
in 'Transactions of the Caernarvonshire
Historical Society', Vol. 20, 1959

HALE, JOHN R.,
'The Early Development of the Bastion –
An Italian Chronology, c 1450–c 1534',
Europe in the late Middle Ages,
ed. J. R. Hale,
London 1965

HALÉVY, DANIEL,
Vauban: Builder of Fortresses,
transl. Major C. J. C. Street,
London 1924

HALTER, A.,
*Histoire Militaire de la place forte de
Neuf-Brisach*,
Strasbourg 1962

HARVEY, JOHN,
*English Medieval Architects: a Biographical
Dictionary down to 1550*,
Boston (Mass.) 1954

HENNEBERT, Lt-Col,
*L'Art Militaire et la Science: Le Matériel de
Guerre Moderne*,
Paris 1884

HERMENT, Général,
L'Etat des Fortresses belges,
Paris 1913

HINDLEY, GEOFFREY,
Castles of Europe,
London 1968

HMSO,
*Handbook for the R.M.L. 17·72 inch 100-ton
Gun (Mark 1) mounted on sliding carriage and
platform Land Service, 1887*,
HMSO, London 1887

HOGG, OLIVER F. G.,
English Artillery, 1326–1716,
London 1963

HORST DE LA CROIX
*The Literature on Fortification in
Renaissance Italy*, in 'Technology and
Culture 4', Winter 1963
*Military considerations in City Planning –
Fortifications*,
New York 1972

HUGHES, B. P., Major-General,
British Smooth-Bore Artillery,
London 1969

INGLIS, T., Colonel,
*Transporting, Landing and Mounting 80-ton
and 100-ton M.L. Guns, intended for the
Armament of Batteries at Dover, Gibraltar
and Malta*,
War Office, London 1884

JACOBACCI, VITTORIO,
Le fortificazioni austriache di Verona,
in 'Castellum' 2, pp. 99–106,
1965

JERVOIS, Col., RE, CB,
*Coast Defences and the application of iron to
fortification*,
reprint from the 'Journal of the Royal
United Services Institution', Vol. xii, 1868

JONES, HARRY D., Lt-General Sir
*Description of the Russian works at
Bomarsund, in the Åland Islands, and Journal
of the Operations which led to their surrender in
August, 1854, together with observations on the
subject*,
in 'Papers of the Royal Engineers', new
series, Vol. V, 1856
*Reports relating to the re-establishment of the
Fortresses in the Netherlands from 1814 to
1830*,
Printed for private circulation,
London 1861

JONES, JOHN T., Colonel,
*Journals of the Sieges carried on by the Army
under the Duke of Wellington in Spain between
the years 1811 and 1814*,
2 vols, London 1827

*Memoranda relative to the Lines thrown up to
cover Lisbon in 1810*,
London 1829

KENYON, E. R., Major, RE,
Notes on Land and Coast Fortification,
London 1894

KIRKMAN, JAMES,
Fort Jesus, Mombasa,
5th edition, Mombasa 1970

LANGENSKIÖLD, ERIC,
Michele Sanmicheli, The Architect of Verona,
Uppsala 1938

LAWRENCE, A. W.,
Trade Castles and Forts of West Africa,
London 1963

LEVRON, JACQUES,
Le Château fort de la vie au Moyen Age,
Paris 1963

LEWIS, Colonel, RE,
*Report on the Application of Forts, Towers and
Batteries to Coast Defences and Harbours*,
in 'Professional Papers of the Royal
Engineers',
Vol. VII, 1845

LEWIS, EMANUEL RAYMOND,
Seacoast Fortifications of the United States,
Washington (D.C.) 1970

LEWIS, J. F.,
Fortification for English Engineers,
Chatham 1890
*Textbook of Fortification and Military
Engineering*,
Part II, London 1893

LLOYD, E. M.,
*Vauban, Montalembert, Carnot: Engineer
Studies*,
London 1887

MACIVOR, IAN,
*The Elizabethan Fortifications of
Berwick-upon-Tweed*,

in 'Antiquaries Journal', Vol. XLV, 1965
Fort George,
HMSO, Edinburgh 1970

MAGGIORETTI, LEONE A.,
'Architetti e architettura militari', in
L'Opera del genio Italiano all'estero, series 4,
Gli architetti militari,
3 vols, Rome 1933–39

MALTA,
*A Description of Malta, with a sketch of its
history and that of its fortifications, translated
from the Italian, with notes by an officer
resident on the Island*,
Malta 1801

MARCHI, FRANCESCO,
Architettura militare, 5 vols,
ed. Luigi, Marini,
Rome 1810

MARCHINI, GIUSEPPE,
Giuliano da Sangallo,
Florence 1942

MARGA, Le Commandant,
Géographie Militaire,
Paris 1884–85

MAROLOIS, SAMUEL,
The Art of Fortification,
revised by Albert Girard,
Amsterdam 1638

MARSDEN, E. W.,
*Greek and Roman Artillery: Historical
Development*,
London 1969

MELEGARI, VEZIO,
Great Sieges,
London and Glasgow 1970

MEMOIR,
*Memoir on the Fortifications in Western
Germany compiled from various sources*,
in 'Professional Papers of the Royal
Engineers', Vol. II,
1838

MONGOLFIER, BERNARD DE,
Dictionnaire des Châteaux de France,
Paris 1969

MONTGOMERY OF ALAMEIN,
A History of Warfare,
London 1968

MOREL, PIERRE,
The Sights of Carcassonne,
Paris and Grenoble 1951

MULLER, JOHN,
*A Treatise containing the Elementary Part of
Fortification: Regular and Irregular*,
London 1746
A Treatise of Artillery,
London 1759

MULLER-WIENER, W.,
Castles of the Crusaders,
London 1966

NATHAN, M., Lt, RE,
The Fortifications of Verona,
paper XI in 'Professional Papers of the
Royal Engineers Occasional Papers',
Vol. VI, 1881

NEAVERSON, E.,
Mediaeval Castles in North Wales,
London 1947

NIEL, General,
*Siège de Sébastopol: Journal des opérations du
Génie*,
3 vols, Paris 1858

NOLAN, E. H.,
*The Illustrated History of the War against
Russia*,
2 vols, London 1857

NUGENT, CHARLES, Colonel Sir, RE,
Fortification in 'Encyclopaedia
Britannica',
Vol. IX, 9th edition, London 1898

OMAN, C. W. C.,
*The Art of War in the Middle Ages. AD
378–1515*,

revised and edited by John H. Beeler,
Ithaca (New York) 1953
*A History of the Art of War in the Sixteenth
Century*,
London 1937

O'NEIL, B. H. ST J.,
*Dartmouth Castle and other defences of
Dartmouth Haven*,
reprint from 'Archaeologia',
Vol. LXXXV, 1936
'Stefan von Haschenperg, an Engineer to King
Henry VIII, and his work,
in 'Archaeologia', Vol. XCI, 1945
*Castles and Cannon: A Study of Early
Artillery Fortifications in England*,
Oxford 1960

PARSONS, WILLIAM BARCLAY,
'Leonardo da Vinci, the Military
Engineer', in *Engineers and Engineering in
the Renaissance*, Vol. V.
Cambridge (Mass.) & London 1968

PASLEY, C. W.,
*Course of Instruction, Originally Composed for
the use of the Royal Engineers Department*,
London 1814–17

PATTERSON, A. TEMPLE,
'Palmerston's Folly'. *The Portsdown and
Spithead Forts*,
Portsmouth 1970

PAYNE-GALLWEY, RALPH, Sir,
The Crossbow,
New York 1958

PEROGALLI, CARLO,
Castelli della pianura lombarda,
Milan 1960

PERROT, GEORGES, & CHIPIEZ,
CHARLES,
Histoire de l'Art dans L'Antiquité,
Vol. VI, *La Grèce Primitive*,
Paris 1894

PETERSON, HAROLD L.,
The Book of the Gun,
London 1968

PHILIPS, G., Colonel,
Text Book of Field Engineering,
London 1901

PLESSIX, H., & LEGRAND-GIRARDE, E.,
Manuel complet de Fortification,
3rd ed, Paris & Nancy 1900

POPE, DUDLEY,
Guns,
London 1955

PORTER, WHITWORTH,
History of the Corps of Royal Engineers,
2 vols, London 1889

POUNCEY, PHILIP,
*Girolamo da Treviso in the Service of
Henry VIII*, in 'Burlington Magazine',
Vol. XCV, 1953

PRO CIVITATE,
*Plans en relief de villes belges, levés par des
ingénieures militaires français – XVII –XIX
Siècle,*
Brussels 1965

PROMIS, CARLO,
*Biografie di ingegneri militari italiani dal
secolo XIV alla meta del XVIII,*
Turin 1874

REVLEAUX, FRANCESCO,
*Le Grandi Scoperte: Le arti. I, macchine,
artiglierie, armi,*
Turin 1891

REY, G.,
*Étude sur les monuments de l'Architecture
Militaire des Croisés en Syrie,*
Paris 1871

REYEN, PAUL E. VAN,
Middeleeuwse Kastellen,
Bussum 1971

RITTER, GERHARD,
The Schlieffen Plan,
transl. A. & E. Wilson,
London 1958

ROBINSON, G. T.,
The Fall of Metz,
London 1871

RONZANI, FRANCESCO, & LUCIOLLI,
GIROLAMO,
*Le fabbriche civili, ecclesiastiche e militari di
Michele Sanmicheli,*
Verona 1832

ROWE, VIVIAN,
*The Great Wall of France: the triumph of the
Maginot Line,*
London 1959

RUSSELL, WILLIAM HOWARD,
*General Todleben's History of the Defence of
Sebastopol: 1854–5: A Review,*
London 1865
*Russell's Despatches from the Crimea –
1854–56,*
ed. Nicolas Bentley,
London 1970

SANDES, E. W. C., Lt-Colonel,
The Military Engineer in India,
Vol. I, Chatham 1933

SAUNDERS, A. D.,
'Palmerston's Follies' – A centenary,
'Journal of the Royal Artillery',
Vol. LXXXVII, No. 3, Winter 1960
*Hampshire Coastal Defence since the
Introduction of Artillery,*
in 'Archaeological Journal',
Vol. CXXIII, May 1967

SCHELIHA, VON,
A Treatise on Coast-Defence,
London 1868

SCHUKKING, W. H.,
De Oude Vestingwerken van Nederland,
Amsterdam 1941

SÉBASTOPOL,
Guerre d'Orient: Siège de Sébastopol,
Paris & Strasbourg 1859

SELLMAN, R. R.,
Castles and Fortresses,
London 1954

SIMPSON, W. DOUGLAS,
Castles from the Air,
London 1949
Castles in England and Wales,
London 1969

SMAIL, R. C.,
Crusading Warfare – 1097–1193,
Cambridge 1956

SMITH, GEORGE, Captain,
An Universal Military Dictionary,
London 1779

SORRELL, ALAN
Living History,
London 1965

STAVELEY, T. K.,
Notes on Brixen and Verona in 1838,
in 'Professional Papers of the Royal
Engineers', Q, Vol. IV, 1842

STRAITH, HECTOR, Major,
Treatise on Fortification and Artillery,
revised by Thomas Cook &
John T. Hyde
7th ed, London 1858

TAIT, A. A.,
The Protectorate Citadels of Scotland,
in 'Architectural History', Vol. 8, 1965

THOMPSON, A. HAMILTON,
*Military Architecture in England during the
Middle Ages,*
London 1912

TOY, SIDNEY,
*A History of Fortification from 3000 BC to
AD 1700,*
London 1955

TUULSE, ARMIN,
Castles of the Western World,
transl. R. P. Girdwood,
London 1958

VAUBAN, SEBASTIEN LE PRESTRE DE,
*The New Method of Fortification as
practised by Monsieur de Vauban,
Engineer-General of France,*
6th edition, by A.S., London 1762

VILLENA, LEONARDO,
*Sull'apporto italiano alla fortificazione con
baluardo,*
in 'Castellum', 4, pp. 81–92, 1966

VIOLLET-LE-DUC, E.,
*Essay on the Military Architecture of the
Middle Ages,*
transl. M. Macdermott,
Oxford & London 1860
Annals of a Fortress,
transl. by Benjamin Bucknall,
London 1875
*Description et histoire du Château de
Pierrefonds,*
Paris 1877
La Cité de Carcassonne,
Paris 1878
Description du Château de Coucy,
Paris 1880

VITRUVIUS,
The Ten Books of Architecture,
transl. Morris Hicky Morgan,
New York 1960

WARD, B. R., Major, RE,
Notes on Fortification: with a synoptical chart,
London 1902

WEBSTER, GRAHAM,
The Roman Army,
Chester 1956

WEISSMULLER, ALBERTO A.,
Castles from the Heart of Spain,
London 1967

ZASTROW, A. DE,
Histoire de la Fortification Permanente,

transl. from German into French by
Duparcq (ed. de la Barre), 2 vols and
atlas, Paris 1856

In addition there are many valuable
guides and monographs on individual
forts and castles published in Britain by
the Department of the Environment, in
Canada by the St Lawrence Parks
Commission and in the United States by
the National Park Service.

INDEX